DATE DUE

RELIGION'S REBEL SON

LLOYD BILLINGSLEY

RELIGION'S REBEL SON

Fanaticism in Our Time

MULTNOMAH · PRESS

Portland, Oregon 97266

By the same author:
  Nonfiction:
    The Generation that Knew Not Josef
    The Absence of Tyranny
  Fiction:
    A Year for Life
  Plays:
    Green Card
    Royal Suite

The author wishes to thank Randall Kuhl for his assistance and encouragement in the preparation of this book.

RELIGION'S REBEL SON
© 1986 by Lloyd Billingsley
Published by Multnomah Press
Portland, Oregon 97266

Printed in the United States of America

Library of Congress Cataloging-in-Publication Data

Billingsley, Lloyd.
  Religion's rebel son.

  Includes index.
  1. Fanaticism. I. Title.
BR114.B54   1986   291.4'2   86-16311
ISBN 0-88070-139-0

86 87 88 89 90 91 – 10 9 8 7 6 5 4 3 2 1

Dedicated to my parents,
Kenneth Billingsley and Victoria Billingsley,
who gave so much, and got so little.

CONTENTS

The red, red blood splatters the cities and plains
of the Cambodian fatherland,
The sublime blood of the workers and peasants,
The blood of revolutionary combatants of both sexes.
                              —First three lines of the national
                              anthem of Democratic Kampuchea

The age of enlightenment was also an age of fanaticism.
                              —Ronald Knox

INTRODUCTION
An Age in Search of a Name

Like Adam, twentieth-century man is fond of naming things, although today he finds time periods much more to his taste than animals. He loves to cram bundles of years into a file drawer, slam it shut, and stick on his own label. For example, the seventies were proclaimed the Me Decade, as though egotism and narcissism had been suspended during the supposedly altruistic, radical sixties, and might be lifted again in the sleek, computerized eighties—the dawn of the Information Age.

In naming any time period, selective amnesia seems to be the rule. The thirties were thus the Depression Era, not the National Socialist Era or Decade of the Great Purges. Though the fifties were packed with change, discovery, and for the most part, peace, revisionist academics and journalists are fond of referring to them as the McCarthy Era, or Cold War Years; both, in their minds, contemporary versions of the ever-famous Dark Ages.

Likewise, feminists and Marxists often refer to the bulk of human civilization—at least until the advent of enlightened people like themselves—as "sexist" and "bourgeois" respectively. For all who equate change and progress, history serves as a convenient treason trial.

And then there is the United Nations, that great *pons asinorum* on the Hudson, announcing to the masses the "International Year of the Child" or what have you, the primary benefit of such proclamations often being not better treatment for children, the handicapped, etc., but a special issue of postage stamps in many countries.

Examining the current century, and the various labels it has been given, one can easily conclude that all labels fall short of the mark. Though Dietrich Bonhoeffer believed, contrary to much evidence, that mankind had come of age, it would perhaps be possible to designate modern times as the Century of the Child, a long, destructive tantrum due to some mysterious *El Niño* effect. Or in Maoist terms, The Great Leap Backward, since the New Class has launched a comeback for feudalism, with much free advertising in the Western press. Malcolm Muggeridge, flying in the face of *soi-disant* progressives, sees a death wish in the guise of liberalism as the dominant motivating force in the Western world. His description of the seventies as the Decade of the Great Liberal Death Wish[1] would do quite nicely for the last seventy years, with some variations.

Why has Century of the Fanatic[2] seldom been nominated as the best description of our age? It seems most appropriate, for fanatics—not moderate men of reason and good faith—have been ascendant, particularly in politics. Thus placed, they touch us all.

The utopian Golden Age envisioned by nineteenth-century seers like Winwood Reade, Herbert Spencer and H.G. Wells became the arena of a demented, genocidal Austrian and his racist *Reich*; a bloated, megalomaniac Italian who proposed restarting the calendar at his, not Christ's, birth; a (now) glass-encased secular saint who advocated the *liquidation* of entire classes of people; a paranoid Red Tsar who carried out these liquidations with cold, deadly efficiency while simultaneously being venerated in the West; an obscurantist Chinese peasant *qua* Great Helmsman, who plunged nearly a quarter of mankind into what some have jocosely but accurately called the Dung Dynasty; and countless other fanatics like Pol Pot, the Ayatollah Khomeini and Col. Khadafy who have followed in their footsteps, leaving poverty and death in their wake. Their name is legion. Much of this, to be sure, is done in the name of Science, Progress and the Brotherhood of Man. As the latter two cases show, it may also be perpetrated in the name of God.

Then, too, there are terrorists of all stripes, from the neo-Nazi white supremacist Ku Kluckers to the Red Brigades and even the Animal Liberation Front, whose members have issued death threats to research scientists who experiment with animals. One cannot leave out macabre characters like Reverend Jim Jones and Charles Manson, for their cases are different from, say, Hitler only in degree, not in kind. Nor can one forget the crowd of American youths in Cincinnati who, in their zeal to enter a concert staged by a popular band, trampled eleven of their peers to death. One of them later explained, "What would you do if you paid eleven dollars for a ticket?" Recognized or not, fanaticism is the spirit of our age.

One would think that such sweeping trends would be readily identified, diagnosed, and even opposed by contemporary sages who make it their business to tell the world what is going on—for example, high-profile sociologists, politicians, clergy, and revered media "anchorpersons," like the *abbé* Dan Rather, who, equipped with journalism degrees, million-dollar salaries, makeup, and the latest technology, purport to interpret the world through Bigger and Better News with an accuracy not available before the invention of the satellite and teleprompter. What most often emerges is not truth but a kind of *Newzak*, information entertainment with content very close to a snuff-film, and often as abstract and fragmented as a rock video. The camera's lens does not readily admit light; its angle is narrow; and—something often forgotten—someone must decide where to aim it. Though pictures tell a thousand words, quite often they are all false. As Blake wrote, they ever must believe a lie, who see with, not through, the eye. It was for reasons like these that Jesus, in *The Fourth Temptation*, refused the devil's offer of free prime-time television to promote Christianity.[3] He knew the film editors could make him appear however they pleased.

Footage of fanaticism at work—terrorist hijackings for example—is the stuff of television newsmen's wildest dreams. Like *Star Wars* director George Lucas, they want "action," stuff that will "play," make the folks at home take notice, and most of all, boost those important Nielsen ratings on which advertisers base their spending. Extremists like the Islamic *Jihad* group know full well that they are virtually guaranteed television coverage; their actions, accordingly, are carefully crafted pieces of political theatre, aired free of charge. Though somber news readers, eyes darting from camera to teleprompter, may inveigh against violence, by turning such incidents into after-dinner thrills for the excitement-starved masses, media bosses only encourage the very thing they decry.

That academics have failed to identify fanaticism as the engine of our time is not all that surprising. After all, some learned scholars have insisted for years that a misanthropic *enragé* who sat in the reading room of the British Museum was the fount of all wisdom, and the economic determinism and class struggle he advocated as much a matter of scientific fact as the boiling point of water or the elevation of Katmandu. As Paul Johnson has pointed out, the social sciences, far from offering answers or solutions, are often very much a part of the problem.[4]

The truth is, in a conformist age, fanatics are not always dreaded, but are frequently admired. They are the men of action who set out to hammer the world into the image of their own ideas, even if it means razing the present. They are the stuff of history. The scholarly man of ideas who spends his life in the quiet alcoves of a library or holding forth in front of students frequently venerates those who actively experiment in the human laboratory, even if this activity is mostly demolition, not construction. Hence, fanatical activists have often heard cheers, not criticism, from the Academy.[5]

Likewise in the print media, those who cover the news are often consumed with admiration for those who make it, especially people who frequently mention "social justice" and are out to establish an egalitarian socialist millenium. Charles Krause, chronicler of the absurd massacre in Guyana ("a mass suicide for the glory of socialism,"[6] as Jones put it, unconsciously providing what may turn out to be the world's epitaph) admits his great reluctance to believe the considerable evidence of the nefarious, perverted reality of Jones and his commune. "The truth was," he writes with refreshing candor, "that I rather admired Jim Jones's goals. . . . It seemed to me that the People's Temple had a legitimate purpose, a noble purpose, and was more or less succeeding."[7] When the bullets began to fly and people to pile up in dead heaps like tropical insects around a lamp, he realized that he had been "stupid."[8] The ideological fungus on his journalistic retina prevented him from identifying a dangerous fanatic, and very nearly cost him his life. He was not the only one to err so egregiously; the *Los Angeles Herald* named Jones "Humanitarian of the Year" in 1976. This same blinding fungus often affects those in government ranks, whose job it is to protect us.

Jones was openly courted by Rosalynn Carter during the 1976 presidential campaign. Politicians like California's (then) Lieutenant Governor Mervyn Dymally visited Jonestown and returned home with praise. Bella Abzug, Walter Mondale, and Hubert Humphrey offered their endorsement.[9] When it comes to fanaticism, those in the corridors of power have also paid their respects.

For the elusive "average" person, the situation is analogous. Western countries are affluent, and affluence breeds boredom. The West is becoming a civilization of *voyeurs*. For those who spend a sizable percentage of their lives getting vicarious kicks by looking at television, the appeal of zealots ready to kill and die for a cause is undeniable. For any kind of fanatical activist to gain a following, or at least admiration, is not a difficult matter. The situation in the church is no better, and may be worse.

In ecclesiastical circles, all one need do to be considered profound ("deeply concerned about justice and social issues") is to become a rice Marxist.[10] One need only announce that, after much careful study and travail of soul, one has discovered that Socialism and Christianity are basically the same thing, and that Marxist-Nihilist revolutionaries or genocidal Socialist dictators, far from constituting any sort of threat as conservatives insist, are actually ushering in the Kingdom of Heaven on Earth.[11] To cite just one example, Latin American Communist guerrillas who die in the struggle to establish new seventh-rate tyrannies like Cuba are credited by Protestant theologian José Míguez Bonino with fulfilling the words of Christ found in John 15:13: "Greater love has no man than this, that a man lay down his life for his friends."[12] Bonino is also "deeply impressed" with Stalin, because his "depth" and "seriousness" remind him of Puritan concentration on "the one thing that matters."[13]

Rev. William Sloane Coffin's Riverside Church in New York City was the scene of a memorial service for Miss Sandy Pollack, a high-profile activist of the Communist party USA. The Rev. Coffin said in his eulogy, "Sandy did not believe in God, but God believed in Sandy."[14] (One wonders how the Reverend gained access to this information.) This kind of clerical claptrap in favor of socialism and its shock troops comes when socialism is being acknowledged by some of its most ruthless practitioners as useless and a failure. On February 20, 1985, Hu Yaobang of the Chinese Communist party stated that his countrymen had "wasted twenty years in radical leftist nonsense."[15] But the deity of Rev. Coffin and his clones in *Sojourners* magazine and the World and National Council of Churches apparently endorses radical leftist nonsense. It is a dismal situation indeed, but a few have seen things differently.

Not, however, clergymen such as Hewlett Johnson and his imitators, who have composed sycophantic odes to politi-

cal fanatics like Stalin and Mao Tse-tung. Not democrati-
cally- elected and constitutionally-restricted politicians who
still admire the freedom of social experimentation in dic-
tatorships, and who return wide-eyed from dreary gulags
claiming, "They have much to teach us." Not liberal journalists who freely give Jim Jones (but never Margaret
Thatcher) the benefit of the doubt. Not supposedly tuned-in
cultural critics who describe some musical fanatic biting the
heads off bats on stage as "a playful epiphany." Not Western
Man, snug in his domestic Third World of ignorance,
stretched out watching *I Love Lucy* reruns and MTV, and
who thinks Walter Cronkite is "deep." No, it took a sometimes windy and superficial but often clearheaded agnostic
to ignore the cant and to formulate a different analysis.

   The True Believer and *The Passionate State of Mind* by the
late longshoreman/philosopher Eric Hoffer are two of the as-
tonishingly few works on the subject of fanaticism, a void at
which this book is aimed. For the most part antagonistic or
at least indifferent to Christianity, Hoffer may have changed
his mind about God at the end of his life. On his last day
alive he scribbled some lines about repentance and Jesus
Christ, which may or may not be significant. Though every
bit as astute and often more eloquent than establishment
cognoscenti, he was generally disregarded by them, as the *au-
todidacte* often is by the tenured professor. He is a most sympathetic figure; born in poverty, he was nearly blind until age
fifteen. When his eyesight returned he read everything he
could get his hands on, in English and German. When other
migrant workers or stevedores were lurking in bars, Hoffer
was reading Montaigne. Like Arthur Koestler, who noted
that since the Enlightenment the place of God had been vac-
ant in the West, Hoffer presents an essentially religious
analysis of the human dilemma:

> In this godless age, as much as in any preceding religious age,
> man is still preoccupied with the saving of his soul. The dis-
> crediting of established religions by enlightenment did not
> result in a weakening of the religious impulse. A traditional

religion canalizes and routinizes the quest for salvation. When such a religion is discredited, the individual must do his own soul-saving, and he is at it twenty-four hours a day. There is an eruption of fanaticism in all departments of life—in business, politics, literature, art, science, and even in lovemaking and sport. The elimination of the sacerdotal outlet results thus in a general infection and inflammation of the social body. [16]

Here, then, is our situation: an incurably religious creature like man in a secular (and therefore polytheistic) age. The result? A rumbling, fuming Krakatoa of fanaticism.

One can hear the groans from the Academy. What, no graphs? No charts? No demographic analysis? No frustrated libido? The thought that anyone *sans* post-graduate degrees might know something about life or human behavior that they don't seldom crosses their minds. In fact, professors often confuse being an academic with being an intellectual. [17] They are not the same thing.

Television news teams are likewise frustrated. When and where did this happen? Who saw it, and where do they live? How can we film it and show footage before the weather, sports, and Alpo commercials?

Notice, too, that in this view there is no clear villain, which will disappoint Marxists and progressive clergy who so often applaud what Hoffer cites as the problem—the discrediting of traditional religion and the ensuing misapplication of the religious impulse. Modern fanatics and their followers need not believe in God; but they must have an effective devil. If only Mr. Hoffer had blamed the USA, or England, or junk food, or multinational corporations, or nuclear power, then he might have appeared on more talk shows, billed as one "deeply concerned about the human condition."[18]

That individuals and their personal beliefs—especially about God—are in any way responsible for what happens to them is a thought light years away from the modern mind. Thinking and speaking in terms of groups has long been a fashion. Instead of loving one's neighbor—a living, breathing, imperfect human being with a face, disposition, name, and address—love for the abstract "mankind" is demanded. How much easier to love mankind than one's neighbor!

Though few of his contemporaries would agree, Hoffer does have substantial support for his thesis among some in the past who might be described as heavyweights. William Blake noted that, "Man must, and will, have some religion." Pascal expresses this thought in his *Pensées*, number 81: "It is natural for the mind to believe and for the will to love; so that for lack of true objects, they must attach themselves to the false."

Augustine posed the question: "What will satisfy you if God Himself will not?" The answer, it appears, is nothing.

But many questions arise. Could fanaticism be anatomical? A sickness treatable by psychoanalysis or electric shock? Is it a synonym for "extremism"? Is it related to ideology or religion? Or is it a pattern of behavior demonstrated by most people at one time or another? Are religious faith and firm theological convictions the marks of a fanatic, as Hoffer also contended? Is it true that the fervent Christian and the zealous Communist are both the same sort of "True Believer"? What, exactly, is this jealous god that touches us all?

INTRODUCTION, NOTES
1. Malcolm Muggeridge, "The Great Liberal Death Wish," *Things Past* (New York: William Morrow, 1978), 220-38.
2. Bernard-Henri Lévy, author of *Barbarism with a Human Face* and an adviser to French president Francois Mitterand, calls the present an "age of fanatics" in his second book, *The Testament of God* (New York: Harper and Row, 1980), 37.
3. Malcolm Muggeridge, *Christ and the Media* (Grand Rapids: Eerdmans, 1977), 23-42.
4. See Paul Johnson, *Modern Times* (New York: Harper and Row, 1983), 730.
5. "There is a natural connection between the teaching profession and a taste for totalitarian government; prolonged association with the immature—fanatical urchins competing for caps and blazers of distinguishing colors—the dangerous pleasures of over-simple exposition, the scars of the endless losing battle for order and uniformity which rages in every classroom, dispose even the most independent minds to shirt-dipping and saluting." From Evelyn Waugh's, "For Schoolboys Only," in *The Essays, Articles, and Reviews of Evelyn Waugh*, ed. Donat Gallagher (Boston: Little, Brown, 1984), 198.
6. Charles Krause and the Washington Post, *Guyana Massacre: The Eyewitness Account* (New York: Berkley Books, 1978), 79.

7. Ibid., 84.
8. Ibid., 91.
9. Robert D. McFadden, "Leading Americans Backed Jones Sect," *New York Times*, 21 November 1978, p. 16.
10. The reference is to Asians who associated with missionaries not out of an interest in Christianity, but for food.
11. For a study of the Western support and adulation for Socialism in the thirties and the present see: Lloyd Billingsley, *The Generation That Knew Not Josef*, (Portland, Ore.: Multnomah Press, 1985).
12. José Míguez Bonino, *Christians and Marxists, The Mutual Challenge to Revolution*, (Grand Rapids: Eerdmans, 1976), 136.
13. Ibid., 134.
14. See R. Emmett Tyrrell, "The Continuing Crisis" in *The American Spectator*, April 1985, p. 6.
15. Ibid.
16. Eric Hoffer, *The Passionate State of Mind* (New York: Harper and Row, 1954), 86.
17. For an example of this, see Richard Pierard in "The Unmaking of Francis Schaeffer" in *The Wittenburg Door* (April-May 1984, pp. 27-29). Pierard, history professor at Indiana State University, points out that Francis Schaeffer's doctorate was honorary and implies that Schaeffer was somehow intellectually bereft for never experiencing graduate seminars or having to defend a thesis. Moreover, Pierard adds that "academicians and social activists now realize that he (Schaeffer) was not an intellectual but an evangelist." I leave it to the reader to judge which one, Pierard or Schaeffer, has had more intellectual impact on the Christian community. Eric Hoffer never went to school; George Orwell never attended university; Malcolm Muggeridge very nearly failed in his quest for a bachelor's degree. By Pierard's either/or standards, Hoffer is a longshoreman, not an intellectual; Orwell a novelist, not an intellectual; and Muggeridge a journalist, not an intellectual.
18. Hoffer thought that the reason he was ignored was that he criticized socialism and spoke well of the United States.

CHAPTER 1
RELIGION'S REBEL SON

"It's a beautiful thing, the destruction of words."
—Syme, Party Newspeak expert, from Orwell's *1984*

Defining terms in the 1980s is no easy task. The widespread destructiveness so evident in this century has spread to words, with disastrous consequences. At one time, *truth* and *God* were widely understood, whereas now only non-words like *Coca-Cola* are universal. The casualty list of very beautiful words now either dead or maimed beyond recognition is long, including: love, compassion, peace, and even "child," for which the ghastly phrase, "product of conception," is freely substituted. Imagine the reaction of shepherds on the Galilean hills to this announcement: "Behold, a virgin shall conceive and bring forth a product of conception." They might have wondered if these were indeed, "good tidings of great joy." Unlike modern Word Police such as militant feminists, they had no difficulty with "child."

Since an easy way to discredit anyone is to say, "She's a fanatic," this word also gets a good workout, most often without reference to its original meaning. Both the word and concept have become trivialized.

The English term *fanatic* is derived from the Latin *fanaticus*, which means, "inspired by a divinity." It was used of priests and soothsayers, the oracles or intermediaries who formed part of the established order of things in antiquity. Fanaticism had no pejorative connotation until the eighteenth century, when it was most often used by philosophers to denounce religious zealotry, which, in the age of the Inquisition, often needed denouncing.

The root of *fanaticus* is *fanum*, meaning "temple." The English word *profane* is derived from the Latin *profanus*, meaning "before (i.e., "outside of") the temple."

To say that someone is a "religious fanatic"—still the most common usage of the term—is to utter a redundancy, no strange occurrence in an age of "free gifts" and "learning resource centers," known in earlier times simply as libraries.

Fanaticism is a purely religious concept, though fanatics need not be religious people in the traditional sense. To return to Hoffer's analysis, at one time this religious inspiration found expression through channels like the Christian church. But with the onslaught of secularism and the discrediting of traditional religion, the individual was left to his own soul-saving; left also to the mercy of the thousand smirking (or panting) icons hawked everywhere at high decibel levels. Hence, as Hoffer saw it, the eruption of fanaticism in all areas of life and the "religiofication" of the secular. Jacques Ellul similarly writes, "The greatest attempts to destroy religion only result in a new religiousness."[1]

Parents in strongly Roman Catholic countries, for example, might be thought fanatical for giving their children names like *Jesús*, *Jesús-María*, *Concepción* and *Incarnación*. In Stalinist Russia, the world's first atheistic state, people had supposedly progressed beyond this kind of excess; nevertheless, in their secular sensibility some parents still managed to name their sons "Tractor" instead of "Boris" during the collectivization of agriculture, and their daughters "Electricity" instead of, say, "Ludmilla" in homage to Lenin's dictum, "Soviet power plus electricity equals Communism." And imagine a slightly squeamish child having to grow up, as some did, being called "Obligation," in honor of the socialist work ethic. Such a tag would surely be a cruel curse, a mark of Cain. It was not until 1971 that Soviet citizens were allowed to change these abominations.[2] When you examine both cases, which demonstrates fanaticism? Jesús and María, at least, are genuine names. Ellul seems right about the new religiousness.

Fanaticism is what happens when people try, in the spiritual sense, to save themselves. Zeal and allegiance once reserved for God are now freely accorded to just about anything. The eager acolytes are called "fans," a derivation of "fanatic." What shows the religious nature of contemporary society more than thousands of supposedly sensible, educated youths paying three-figure prices to prostrate themselves in craven adoration before popular singers? Not only does this happen, but multitudes pattern their speech, dress, and personal ethics in fastidious obedience to their objects of devotion. This is nothing new, of course. Elvis once had them screaming in the aisles; now, pilgrims visit his grave. The continued attention given him seems a form of ancestor worship. Similarly, mass-produced (and purchased) dolls of mega-hyped entertainers like Michael Jackson could well be considered icons. If this is not fanaticism in its true religious sense, it is hard to imagine what might be. The obviously phony name of one venerated heartthrob seems intended by its inventors to exploit this very thing. The young man in question has a flair for chains and leather; his name is, yes, Billy Idol.

Of course, devotees of Billy Idol or The Who (the band eleven people died trying to see) would vehemently deny their devotion is fanatical, even after helping trample a dozen people to death at a concert. (What would you do if you paid eleven dollars for a ticket?) In fact, all one need do to be called a fanatic is to suggest to a star-struck fan that some posturing, platitude-bleating millionaire businessperson of dubious sex and little talent is less worthy of attention than, say Jesus Christ, or even Duke Ellington.

Dictionary definitions, so often inadequate, do shed some light. In entries on the term *fanaticism*, the word *credulity* appears a lot, expecially relating to religious matters. *Vehemence, hatred,* and *violence* are also frequently mentioned. Some call fanaticism a perversion of enthusiasm by hatred. Others associate fanaticism with a particular type of person: adherents of cure-all utopian schemes.

It would be facile to think, as some eighteenth-century French philosophers did, that any kind of person or group has a monopoly on fanaticism. To the French revolutionaries it meant simply "Catholicism." Effigies were made of it and burned. Catholic religious objects were placed on donkeys and mocked. There was not a speech where fanaticism was not mentioned and denounced. Statues were erected to its victims. And yet, true to form, the revolutionaries themselves remain a beacon to fanatics through the centuries, having set the highest of standards.

We think Pol Pot's order to evacuate Phnom Penh, whose inhabitants he then proceeded to butcher in large numbers, was nearly incomprehensible in its barbarity. We are right in thinking so. But we must not forget that the zealous Jacobins decreed that Lyons, the second largest city in France, was to be utterly destroyed, and its name struck from the list of cities of the Republic.[3] They predicted that future travelers would say, "and Lyons was over there."

Without doubt, all of us at times display credulity in religious matters (whether in secular or traditional religions) and vehemence toward our opponents. If there exists any kind of "spark" in all of us, it may well be the one that kindles fanaticism, not reasonable faith. As history shows, fanaticism often perverts the true service of God; and therein lies the key to the concept, very much along the lines advanced by Hoffer.

François Marie Arouet was otherwise known as Voltaire. (One wonders, was he ashamed of "Marie," which the French and Spanish give to boys, like later Russians were of "Tractor?") He thought and wrote much about fanaticism, authoring a play, *Fanaticism, or Mahomet the Prophet*, and an epic poem on the subject, *La Henriade*, which states, among its 4,330 lines:

> Discord, attentive, heard his hideous cries,
> And swift to Pluto's dreary regions flies.
> From those dark realms, the worst of tyrants came
> Fanatic demon is his horrid name
> *Religion's son, but rebel in her cause*
> He tears her bosom and disdains her laws.[4]

(italics added)

In his *Philosophical Dictionary*, Voltaire departs from the poetic and seems to lean toward the medical model. He calls fanaticism a "gangrene of the brain," "a sickness of the people," and, "a heavenly epilepsy," among other descriptions.[5]

While this pathological aspect is doubtless legitimate,[6] it seems to me at best secondary to the religious dimension. For too long, psychology and psychiatry have supplanted religion as an analytical tool.

Since fanaticisms and fanatics are many and varied, any simple definition must be incomplete. It is true that, as Hoffer said, there are eruptions of fanaticism in every dimension of life, but one must at least try for some sort of precise meaning. In the contemporary scene, fanaticism often takes the form of activated superstition.

Superstitions are unreasonable beliefs and fears of all sorts.[7] As Edmund Burke put it, they are the religions of feeble minds. They are ersatz deities that people serve in pursuit of their own salvation. Some of these deities are more demanding than others. In studying fanaticism, there is likewise a sense of priorities.

In many cases, when a person sets out to save herself through hero-worship, drugs, exercises, etc., the ensuing fanatical behavior affects only her. But too many fanatics not only strive to save themselves; they want to save the world and the rest of us with it—even if we don't want to be saved. It is with such ones that we must be primarily concerned. Taking a cue from Hoffer, who titled his work on the subject *The True Believer*, we shall call them The True Fanatics.

CHAPTER 1, NOTES
1. Jacques Ellul, *The New Demons* (New York: Seabury, 1975), 131.
2. From a Reuters dispatch, quoted in *Parade Magazine*, 6 January 1985, p. 7. Haynal, in *Fanaticism*, reports that some children were named "Lenin" and "Stalin" and others "First Artillery Regiment."
3. For the entire decree see Gerard de Puymège, *Fanaticism: A Historical and Analytical Study* (New York: Shocken Books, 1983), 98, 99.
4. Voltaire, *La Henriade* in Vol. 21 of *The Works of Voltaire*, trans. William H. Fleming (New York: St. Hubert Guild, 1901), 11.
5. See the articles on fanaticism and dogma in Voltaire's *A Philosophical Dictionary* (London: John and Henry L. Hunt, 1824).
6. That there is a mental health dimension to fanaticism cannot be denied. For a psychoanalytical study see Andre Haynal in *Fanaticism* (New York: Shocken Books, 1983), 34-78.
7. The distinction between established religions like Christianity and superstition is maintained even by officially atheistic Marxist governments such as that of mainland China.

PART

1

THE TRUE FANATIC
A Family Album

CHAPTER 2
MAN-GODS AND THEOCRATS

In the biblical Incarnation, the Word of God became Man. In theological terms, Jesus Christ underwent a *kenosis*, a self-emptying. The character of God is thus revealed to his creatures. The apostle John described Christ, the Word made flesh, as "full of grace and truth." This is what happened when God became man; a humbling, a voluntary setting aside of power and privilege. When man becomes god, however, the exact opposite takes place.

Man never becomes so arrogant, so vain, so capable of any lie or fathomless depth of atrocity as when he arrogates divine prerogatives to himself. The True Fanatic is a theocrat, someone who sees himself as acting on behalf of some super-personal force: the Race, the Party, History, the Proletariat, the Poor, and so on. These absolve him from evil, hence he may safely do anything in their service. In rare cases, he thinks he *is* God.

But since it is difficult for anyone to assume the divine role while the genuine item is around, from the crucifixion onward there have been serious attempts to rid the world of God. Bernard-Henri Lévy noted:

From Robespierre to Mao, there is no totalitarianism without this insistent, pathological, obsessive reference to slaying the one and sovereign God.[1]

These efforts, of course, are all doomed to failure; all
the more reason to expect continued fanatical efforts aimed
at extirpating religion. The more impossible the task, the
greater the degree of fanaticism. This seems to be a consistent principle. Commenting on atheistic indoctrination in
Marxist countries, Catholic priest Jerzy Popieluszko noted:

It has been decided in postwar Poland that the young generation is to be educated without God. But it has been forgotten
that God has no duty whatsoever to comply with anyone's
resolutions.[2]

Such remarks ultimately cost him his life. He was
beaten to death by Polish secret police.

Modern theocrats are recruited not from among God's
worshipers, but from his murderers.[3] Having murdered God,
albeit metaphorically, and themselves being disposed to die
for their cause, can these people be expected to tread softly
with their enemies? Theocrats regularly use murder as an instrument of their political policy.[4] They describe this in religious terms: salvation, purging, regeneration, and, above
all—vengeance.

French psychiatrist André Haynal defines a fanatic as
one who has no qualms about violating the homicide taboo.[5]
This willingness to kill for a cause is one of many similarities
among history's worst fanatics. But there are many others.

Little People

What do Charles Manson, Josef Stalin, Lenin, and
Hitler all have in common? Much, as will be seen. But to a
man they were small and of scant physical distinction.

Arthur Koestler, who, as a zealous Communist wrote
unctuous love-poems about Stalin's Five-Year Plan, was also
notoriously short. This gave him an inferiority complex described by a friend as being of cathedral proportions. There

can be no doubt that the same standard applies in the family of fanatics.

In addition to being short, Hitler was the third son of the third marriage of an Austrian civil servant who was born out of wedlock and who for most of his life went by the rather comic last name of Shicklgruber. Hitler also had some potentially embarrassing physical defects.[6]

During the murder trials for the Tate-La Bianca killings, Charles Manson's photo made front pages all over the world. While sensational press coverage, including Nixon's careless public remarks about his guilt, made Manson seem a monster larger than life, it rarely if ever emerged that he stood barely five-foot two. An examination of his life makes it clear that he most definitely did not, as pop psychology has it, "feel good about himself."

Manson is a perfect example of someone substituting delusions of power for his own lack of stature. Saber at his side, he charged about the desert in a Volkswagen dune buggy, imagining himself to be Rommel, the commander of Hitler's African forces.[7] Manson also thought Hitler was, "a tuned-in guy who leveled the karma of the Jews."[8]

Imagine the delight of dumpy little peasant boy Mao Tse-tung when finally conferred with immortality by the teeming Chinese masses and a credulous Western intelligentsia. Imagine him staring at a poster of himself ten meters square. Picture him uttering Machiavellian banalities like "Power comes from the barrel of a gun," and watching sycophantic Westerners like Anna Louise Strong reach for their note pads to record what they thought were drippings of pure enlightenment. How all that must have made up for being the little guy on the block!

In the case of Stalin, one notes that he was not only short, but came from the small, obscure region of Georgia, a backwater to the dominant Russians. Doubtless, he heard versions of the biblical joke: "Can any good thing come out of Nazareth?"[9] in regard to his own home turf, since the seminary where he studied was as much an instrument of Russification as it was of learning. How "Little Joe,"[10] as he signed his poems, must have loved to rub it in once he attained what amounted to divine status.

In the struggle for power shown by people like Lenin, Stalin, and others, one can clearly discern the little browbeaten boy seeking a glorious opportunity to wreak vengeance on the big bullies who tormented him during childhood. That some adopted Marxism is no accident: Marxism is attractive to all power-seekers because it offers total and permanent control until such time as the state, as Marx predicted, shall wither away. This is the event that never happens; indeed, it cannot. Imbued with total authority, the little people have rarely missed their chance to get in their licks. The corridors of power are full of them. The ruling bureaucrats in Orwell's 1984 are not tall, Aryan types, but "little beatle-like men."

One can make too much of the issue of size. But smallness can help fuel a megalomania when because of it an inferiority complex is nurtured. Clearly, in the past, fanatical means have been freely used to repair such complexes. But the individual fanatics are not small in strictly physical terms.

Feet of Clay

Fanatics are often people who have attempted to produce art and failed. This failure helped to launch their extremist careers. Many of the Nazi elite had deep artistic ambitions. By all standards, most failed miserably.[11] Hitler was twice rejected by the Vienna Academy of Fine Arts, but to the end of his life referred to himself as an artist.

The arts, particularly literature, are a kind of middle ground, a current that runs between the two poles of mysticism and activism. With mysticism eliminated by secular ideology, and with the middle ground of imaginative art beyond reach, the fanatic is left with activism as a sort of last resort to find meaning in life. He turns to it with desperation. Once putting his hand to the plow, he does not look back.

In a position of power, the artistic failure can take his vengeance.[12] He can, as Hitler did, persecute former critics—in his case, Jews. He can insure that only didactic, orthodox novels are published; or, like the practice of Pol Pot, ensure that no novels or books of any sort are published at all. But the theocrat most often uses art for his own ends. The crass art of the Nazi regime, and the Socialist Realism of the Soviets, are two examples of this.

When Nazi filmmakers like Leni Riefenstahl used their medium for hagiography, they found favor with the rulers by complimenting the "star." This could be described as National Socialist Realism. The Soviet model of this is closely related. This should come as no surprise, since Soviet expansionism is merely a balalaika version of National Socialist *Lebensraum*.

Under Socialist Realism—the only artistic standard allowed in the USSR and all its wholly-owned subsidiaries—if a writer has authored a novel containing accurate descriptions of any kind of shabby conditions, he is told something like the following: "Comrade, it will take two years for your book to be edited and to pass the censors. By that time there will be new factories, new apartments and new roads. Why not, then, write about them as already existing?"

Under such conditions art can only be used to praise a given situation or to attack opponents. Thus constrained, it can have no value at all. The true artists who find satisfaction in their work shun politics, tell the truth, and most often end up in labor camps, exile, or an early grave. Bulgarian writer Georgi Markov turned his powers of satire against the Dictatorship of the Proletariat in his own country. Though living in England at the time, he was murdered. Evidence points to an assassination.

On a smaller scale, much of Charles Manson's anger at the "establishment" can be traced to his rejection as a singer. Though Manson practiced the guitar for hours in jail (where he spent most of his life) and wrote numerous songs, his one-time friend Dennis Wilson of the Beach Boys thought he "never had a musical bone in his body."[13] When his songs failed to kindle enthusiasm, Manson would sulk and hit people. Unable to convey his apocalyptic message through lyrics, he turned to more macabre schemes.

Of fanatical terrorists like the Red Brigades and Baader Meinhoff group, Claire Sterling comments: "The very density of their prose betrays a hopeless incapacity to communicate by any means save the barrel of a gun."[14]

Underachievers

Besides being, in general, failures in the realm of creative endeavor, political fanatics are seldom fully competent at anything. For them, practical experience is a positive impediment. Rarely, if ever, can they be described as legitimate experts, though it often happens, as in Lenin's case, that they elicit the word "genius," another nearly meaningless term in current usage.

One is struck by the half-baked nature of Lenin's academic efforts. His much-exaggerated facility always lay in the realm of theory, not practice. He was all antennae, and no head. He earned good marks in languages, but had no facility for speaking them.[15] He passed his legal exams having done all the study on his own, but was a notoriously poor lawyer.[16] The eight or nine peasants and workers he defended in court were all found guilty. Such a person is not likely to enjoy a thriving law practice. He was even a poor chess player, which might be insignificant anywhere but Russia, where chess is a national passion.[17]

Though Hitler was clever and possessed oratorical gifts, Albert Speer described him as amateurish in many ways, particularly in his pretensions to architectural knowledge.[18] His poor study habits led to a scholastic record described only as "adequate."[19]

Josef Vissarionovich Djugashvili, also known as Stalin, knew how to get what he wanted and read widely. But there is no doubt that, even compared to other True Fanatics, he was at best second-rate.[20] This perhaps explains why he was attracted to utter phonies like the biologist Lysenko. Only in the highly competitive field of political murder is Stalin in any sense distinguished.

Mao Tse-tung is an example of someone with practically no distinction of any sort—physical, artistic, intellectual or otherwise. He is a case of the foolish confounding the more foolish. Paul Johnson describes him as a "coarse, brutal, earthy and ruthless peasant."[21] When one examines his life and many of the statements he made, his fathomless ignorance and, on many occasions, plain stupidity, become clear. The vicious persecution of the educated during the Cultural Revolution probably has as much to do with Mao's own mental shortcomings as anything else.

Again on a smaller scale, the Reverend Jim Jones was a scholastic and intellectual Lilliputian. Though his life is not well-documented, satisfaction with his job cannot have been one of his strong points. He financed his first church by the rather bizarre trade of selling live monkeys on the side, not a job someone with an ego as gargantuan as Jones's is likely to brag about or include on a résumé. Jones's fanaticism could well have been fueled by jokes made about his occupation, perhaps by fellow ministers or even parishioners.[22]

Giangiacomo Feltrini, millionaire publisher and bankroller of European terrorists, was likewise intelligent but theoretical; that is, isolated from mainstream society. He was an odd-looking man, sexually impotent, guilt-stricken, and incompetent in practical areas.[23] This incompetence cost him his life; he blew himself to pieces trying to dynamite an electric pylon.

CHAPTER 2, NOTES
   1. Bernard-Henri Lévy, *The Testament of God* (New York: Harper and Row, 1980), 89.
   2. From a sermon delivered in St. Stanislaw Kotska Church, September 25, 1983.
   3. Lévy, p. 37.

4. Gérard de Puymège in *Fanaticism: A Historical and Psychoanalytical Study* (New York: Shocken Books, 1983), 201.

5. André Haynal in *Fanaticism: A Historical and Psychoanalytical Study* (New York: Shocken Books, 1983), 218.

6. Hitler was a monorchid; he had only one testicle. While neither Hitler's fanaticism, nor anyone else's is anatomical, this defect coupled with disturbed family relations can cause extreme mental imbalances. See Eugene H. Methvin "Hitler and Stalin, Twentieth-Century Super Killers," *National Review*, 31 May 1985, 27.

7. Vincent Bugliosi, Curt Gentry, *Helter Skelter: The True Story of the Manson Murders*, (New York: Norton, 1974), 125.

8. Ibid., 236.

9. John 1:46.

10. Isaac Deutscher, *Stalin, A Political Biography* (Middlesex: Penguin Books, 1966), 36.

11. Eric Hoffer, *The True Believer* (New York: Harper and Row, 1951), 132.

12. George Orwell notes that, "German literature practically disappeared during the Hitler regime." See Orwell's *Inside the Whale and Other Essays* (Middlesex: Penguin Books, 1962), 170.

13. Bugliosi, 251.

14. Claire Sterling, *The Terror Network* (New York: Holt, Rinehart and Winston, 1981), 9.

15. Robert Payne, *The Life and Death of Lenin* (New York: Avon books, 1964), 60.

16. Ibid., 98. See also Bertram D. Wolfe, *Three Who Made a Revolution* (New York: Delta Books, 1964), 86.

17. See Malcolm Muggeridge, *Chronicles of Wasted Time* (New York: Morrow, 1973), 161.

18. Albert Speer, *Inside the Third Reich* (New York: Avon Books, 1969), 74-77.

19. William Shirer, *The Rise and Fall of the Third Reich* (New York: Simon and Shuster, 1960), 11, 14.

20. Deutscher, 45.

21. Paul Johnson, *Modern Times* (New York: Harper and Row, 1983), 545.

22. Charles Krause, *Guyana Massacre* (New York: Berkley Books, 1978), 28.

23. Sterling, 30.

CHAPTER 3
GODS OF STONE

The True Fanatic is always more preoccupied with demolition than construction, with demonology than philosophy. Thus occupied he must take himself with deadly seriousness. The fields are white to harvest; Rome wasn't burned in a night. There is much still standing that needs to be leveled. As Jim Jones and some radical Anabaptist socialists (politically not nearly so far apart as might be imagined) put it, many "structures of evil" exist. To a fanatic with this sort of vision, nothing is funny. A theocrat who believes himself in charge of a world's salvation finds little, if anything, to laugh about.

The perpetrators of the *Grande Terreur*, the Reign of Terror of the French Revolution, boast impressive resumes in theocratic fanaticism. These gentlemen were not a barrel of laughs. History professor Jeffry Kaplow observed:

> Now it is a fact that humor and revolutionary fervor are never congenial bedfellows. The lack of a sense of humor is doubtless one of the most salient characteristics of the revolutionary. Wit and humor appeared as counter-revolutionary vices. Sadet, a shopkeeper in Lyons, is reported to have said that one should mistrust above all people, "who have wit." The remark is perhaps apocryphal, but it reveals a state of mind that the revolutionaries of the

year 11 would not have denied, for they took life very seriously and attached a quasi-religious significance to words.
They could not have been further removed from the good-
natured tradition of jokes and pleasantries of army life, so
dear to Frenchmen as a rule. A joke was simply not ap-
preciated.[1]

An examination of the writings of contemporary revolutionaries, and those favoring sweeping "structural"
change, leads one to the same conclusion: the lack of humor
is the badge of a fanatic.

While religious people have often been thought dour
killjoys who stalk the earth quenching the mirth of anyone
who might be having fun, the strictest Puritan—used in the
pejorative sense of someone who views all pleasure as sinful—will have a hard time competing with revolutionary
fanatics. In Year 11 of the French Revolution (like Mussolini
they restarted the calendar), the ninth day of Pluvoise (the
month of rain; they changed the names of these, too) a decree was issued against those nefarious items that strike at the
very roots of civil order—playing cards. Article One demanded all citizens to bring any card games to the Revolutionary Committee for burning opposite the Temple of
Reason, the new name for Cathedral of Notre Dame. Article
Two stipulated that anyone found in possession of cards
would be punished to the full extent of the law. This kind of
language generally meant the death penalty.[2] What a pity
that there was no French Civil Liberties Union to protest
such intrusive, Big Brother measures.

The much publicized Lutheran minister Rev. Douglas
Roth wages war against Pennsylvania steel companies,
whom he views as solely responsible for the economic problems of this area. With a hard core of followers, he has ha-
rassed the wives and children of executives while they are at
school and church.[3] A minister who was undergoing training
with Roth in these kinds of "prophetic" techniques finally
broke ranks, because, as he told Ed Bradley of 60 Minutes,
"these people have no sense of humor."

The Old Testament tells us that God laughs.[4] Saints and spendthrifts often do likewise. Many outstanding humorists have been believers: Cervantes, Rabelais, Chaucer, Waugh. But the humor of political fanatics would make a very thin book indeed. Rarely innovative, seldom competent, often frustrated, never experienced, but at the same time seeing themselves as supremely important, the theocrat seldom cracks a smile. Small wonder that there is little to be cheerful about in the precincts where the gods of stone hold sway. As a biblical writer might put it: "and there shall be no joy there; laughter will be wiped from faces. For fanatics shall live and dwell among them, and be their god."

Hatred

True greatness involves the ability to see into the mystery of things. This sense of mystery—of the unexplained and unexplainable—is something that secular, scientific man has largely lost. This can be gauged by the way educated North Americans stand awestruck at cartoons like *Close Encounters of the Third Kind*, regarding these as representing something "deep." Modern, scientific Man views all things as comprehensible, since he is the measure of all things. The great cloud of unknowing presents nothing more than an engineering problem. But mysteries remain.

Perhaps the greatest of these is man and why he acts the way he does. Pascal, in addition to being a true genius in science and mathematics, knew something about this. He pointed out that man is the only creature who avidly pursues ends he knows full well will bring him no happiness. He further saw that many people hold a grudge against reality:

> Man wants to be great, and he finds himself small; he wants to be happy and finds himself miserable; he wants to be perfect and finds himself full of imperfections; he wants to be the object of love and esteem among men and he finds that his faults merit only their aversion and scorn. This situation wherein he finds himself produces the most unjust and most criminal passion which can be imagined; for he conceives a mortal hatred against this truth which blames him and convinces him of his faults.[5]

This mortal hatred against the truth is often expressed as an "insistent, pathological, obsessive reference to slaying the one and sovereign God,"[6] as Bernard-Henri Lévy saw it. The Rev. Jim Jones held no conventional concept of God and spoke of religion in Marxist terms, as an opiate of the people. His attitude to the Deity may be discerned in his wild denunciations of the Bible, which he threw to the ground, trampled underfoot, and called an "idol."[7] Though he thought of himself as a reincarnation of Lenin and Christ, he *hated* God. And the ones who hate God usually hate man also. This hatred has even been expressed in a creedal form by Sergey Gennadiyevich Nechayev, a prototypical nihilist revolutionary and True Fanatic in every sense.

Lenin's biographer, Robert Payne, before at all touching on his subject, dedicates a long chapter to Nechayev, whom he calls "the forerunner." Lenin held boundless admiration for the author of *The Revolutionary Catechism*, which states at one point that the revolutionary

> *should not hesitate to destroy any position, any place, or any man in this world. He must hate everyone and everything in it with* an equal hatred.[8] (italics are in the original)

This was the very material—the "science of destruction"—that Lenin wanted to distribute like gospel tracts. Lenin's own writings are redolent of the same hatred; they are strewn with verbs like *shoot, liquidate, seize, attack, exterminate* and many others. Che Guevara, another ideological descendant of Nechayev, said, "We must develop hatred in order to transform man into a machine for killing."[9] And, in the same vein:

> We must above all keep our hatred alive and fan it to paroxysm. Hate as a factor of struggle, intransigent hate of the enemy, hate that can push a human being beyond his natural limits and make him a cold, violent, selective, and effective killing machine.[10]

All True Fanatics, from the totalitarian rulers of a quarter of mankind all the way down to the American neo-Nazis, are motivated by a virulent hatred. Just as there is a kind of love, *agape*, based solely on the condition of its giver, not the receiver, so the hatred of the fanatic is not governed by whether the objects of his wrath deserve it or not; in fact, they rarely do. The more undeserved a persecution, the more violent it is likely to be. The True Fanatic hates, therefore he acts. He hates with *agape* hatred, because of what he *is*, not because of what his victims deserve. And, as a newsman might say in baleful tones, things are even worse than had been previously thought.

Not only does the True Fanatic make hatred the main item of his creed; he also includes it in his liturgy. In *1984* we read of a daily ritual called the Two Minutes Hate: a shrill whistle halts work everywhere and citizens gather around the telescreens. There, Immanuel Goldstein, the omnipresent enemy of the people, repeats his herersies: freedom of thought, speech, and action. He denounces the dictatorship of the Party. As he does so, the people foam with rage; they shriek, chant, and throw things. The hatred is contagious; even Orwell's hero, Winston Smith, who retains a few generous scraps of humanity, feels a desire to torture, to kill, and to smash in faces with a sledgehammer. When the Hate ends, there is the calm face of Big Brother, triumphant over Goldsteinism.[11] While all this is brilliantly done, Orwell did have some models to work from. Hate liturgy is nothing new.

During the French Revolution, orators like Robespierre and Anacharsis Cloots (a humble man who referred to himself as "Orator of the Human Race") would address throngs of the faithful. Using a hypnotic, incantory style, the leaders would decry the crimes of the *Ancien Régime*, chiefly that they had been less than worshipful of people like the Jacobins. The crowd would repeat after each of these recitations: "What remains to them? Assassination!"[12]

A holiday was also dedicated to "Hatred of Tyrants and Traitors"[13] It was an early version of Orwell's Hate Week. Doubtless, a good time was had by all.

Hitler and his underlings likewise employed a revivalist

42 THE TRUE FANATIC, A FAMILY ALBUM

style of meeting and oratory, a kind of responsive shouting of litanies called out by a leader and punctuated with "Heil Hitler!" Such ceremonies—the Nuremburg rallies for instance—were held at night, with ample use of *son et lumière* for mystical effect. By such means, along with rigorous anti-Semitic propaganda, the *volk* were taught how and whom to hate. Ernst Lissauer penned a nationalist hymn urging hatred towards England.[14]

Mao Tse-tung also had a flair for such liturgies. His own Asian version of Goebbels, Lin Piao, would rant, "Sweep away all devils and evil spirits!" and other slogans, followed by the rhythmic chants of the Red Guards.[15]

The differences between Hitler's "Down with the Jews!"; Mao's excoriation of "Foreign devils"; and Charles Manson's battle cry of "Death to all pigs" are purely ones of style, not substance. In every case, the interior life of the True Fanatic is a crowded but unlocked zoo of carefully fondled hatreds. The liturgy of hatred attempts to spread this condition to a wider social body, often with great success.

CHAPTER 3, NOTES

1. Jeffry Kaplow, *New Perspectives on the French Revolution* (New York: John Wiley and Sons, 1965), 309.
2. For a copy of the entire decree see Gérard de Puymège, *Fanaticism: A Historical and Psychoanalytical Study* (New York: Shocken Books, 1983), 95.
3. See Russell T. Hitt, "What Hath Roth Wrought," *Eternity*, February 1985, 10, 11.
4. Psalm 2:4.
5. Blaise Pascal, *Les Pensées* (Paris: Flammarion 1935), 165.
6. Bernard-Henri Lévy, *The Testament of God* (New York: Harper and Row, 1980), 89.
7. Charles Krause, *The Guyana Massacre* (New York: Berkley Books, 1978), 33.
8. The entire catechism is recorded by Robert Payne in *The Life and Death of Lenin* (New York: Avon Books, 1964), 26-33.
9. Quoted in Jacques Ellul, *Violence* (New York: Seabury Press, 1969), 104.
10. Quoted in Claire Sterling, *The Terror Network* (New York: Holt, Rinehart, Winston, 1981), 8.
11. George Orwell, *1984* (London: Cox and Wyman, 1975), 15-20.
12. Puymège, 99.
13. Ibid., 91.
14. Paul Johnson, *Modern Times* (New York: Harper and Row, 1983), 121.
15. Ibid., 547.

CHAPTER 4
THE SPIRIT-FILLED LIFE

UTOPIANISM

The True Fanatic is never satisfied with the present. It matters little what conditions prevail; he considers them spoiled and inadequate, far short of the utopian visions in his hot-house mind. He has the staying power to fence endlessly with the flaming sword barring the entrance to paradise as described in the book of Genesis. He wants to lead mankind back into the garden, albeit one of his own design. He imagines that he can somehow reverse the Fall, which is just about the only empirically verifiable fact in the "science" of human behavior. Utopias, not the Fall, are illusory.

It might be considered odd that criminals like Charles Manson and Jim Jones should be included with well-known politicians like Stalin, and the whole bunch branded as fanatics. But Manson had as clear a vision of political utopia as did Lenin, kind of an erotic playground, a world-wide harem with the blacks (and, presumably, Jews) in positions of submission, and with himself upon the throne.[1] He read such things into Beatles' songs, Robert Heinlein novels and the book of Revelation in the Bible, much as Lenin reinterpreted Marx. Manson understood the reference to the 144,000 as applying to him and his "family."

Hitler's Reich was based on anti-Semitism and racism. In it, the clean-jawed, fair-haired Aryan *ubermenschen* would oversee the work of the slave *undermenschen* such as Slavs and blacks. The similarities with Manson's imagined utopia are striking.

Jim Jones's egalitarian commune was modeled on the Anabaptist version, the classical utopian socialist blueprint. It was intended to be a world of harmony: all ages, colors, races side by side and shoulder to shoulder; a reign of peace, happiness, and brotherhood forever, in defiance of the evil outside world, ruled by the United States. But in any human venture, *who whom?* applies. That is, who gives orders to whom? This is the central question, as Lenin observed. In the Guyana paradise, Jones gave orders; the others obeyed. Near his jerry-built wooden throne in the jungle, he placed a sign that read: "Those who do not remember the past are condemned to repeat it." No one needed to learn this more than Jones. He had obviously never read of John of Leiden's exploits in Munster, which his Jonestown closely paralleled.

The utopias of fanatics never come, but always lie just out of reach. In fact only a few communes of any description, such as the Amish and Hutterites, have succeeded, and these are more ethnic sub-cultures than communes. The people in them are realists, not fanatics. Moreover, they make no effort to proselytize—and herein lies the difference. The True Fanatic will drag us into his kingdom whether we want to go in or not.

Advocates of utopias generally make light of heaven. From their viewpoint this is understandable. Malcolm Muggeridge has pointed out that a utopia is a place where a different set of people are important, whereas in heaven, everyone is important.[2] Everyone is important in heaven because God rules. But a True Fanatic cannot abide a place where he is not the boss.

INFALLIBILITY

As C.S. Lewis demonstrated at the outset of *Mere Christianity*, everyone likes to be right. Most people are capable, if only on occasion, of heated argument to ensure that things will be seen their way.

Admitting that one is wrong can be painful, but is also evidence of functioning humanity. Koestler, Fischer, Gide and others who chronicled their experiences in *The God That Failed* admitted that they were wrong about Stalin, for whose regime some of them had once been willing to type words of unqualified praise, or even lay down their lives. No such admission emerged from the clergymen who announced that Stalin was bringing in the Kingdom of God on earth.

The fanatic is usually a predictable bore, unable to change either his mind or the subject. The ability to recognize and acknowledge a mistake is where he parts company with mere mortals.

Though Christians have been ridiculed for believing in the infallibility of the Pope, in a creed, or in Scripture, it is seldom realized that everyone has a theory of infallibility: the will of the people; the greatest good for the greatest number; Science; conscience; "whatever feels good"; Inevitable Progress; and so on. The fanatic, too, may imagine that such principles are without error, but tends to view infallibility as lodging in individuals, viz., himself. Orwell's *Animal Farm* provides a parable.

Once the animals had succeeded in banishing Jones and gaining control of the farm, they proceeded to apply the principles of Animalism, using various slogans—"four legs good, two legs bad" and so on—to instruct some of the duller creatures. When the chief pigs, especially Napoleon, were rapidly taking on the characteristics of the despised humans, all ideology boiled down to one simple principle which the sincere and hardworking horse, Boxer, adapted as his personal motto: "Napoleon is always right."

Mein Kampf claims with one voice that, "Hitler is always right." The Thoughts of Chairman Mao can be condensed into, "Mao is always right." Volumes of falsified statistics and hours of shrill propaganda advanced one thought—"Stalin is always right!" Piles of mutilated corpses were how Charles Manson showed he was "right." Jim

Jones's version was, "Mass suicide for the glory of socialism." Though many people say they'd "rather die" than admit a mistake, the fanatic is capable of doing it.

PARANOIA

Of course, if, like Orwell's Napoleon, all these various political pigs are always right, it follows that they must be constantly vigilant against error in their subjects. Uneasy lies the head that wears the crown. What the fanatical theocrat lacks in artistic imagination, he makes up in paranoia. There can be no pluralism, no diversity, no individuality in his kingdom. Such things are, to him, manifestations of evil. Since he claims to know everything from the beginning to the end, can anyone come up with something he did not foresee? (Party functionaries in 1984 are quick to credit Big Brother for an idea that came out of their own heads.) On every hand, so he imagines, are heretics, saboteurs, wreckers, hatching their sinister conspiracies. From such paranoia comes the Purge, the assassination.

During his stint as a correspondent in Moscow, Malcolm Muggeridge wrote an article about the Soviet mania for seeing treachery on every hand. He said that you could say about sabotage in the Soviet Union what Voltaire said about God, that if it did not exist, somone would have to invent it. The article was smuggled out, avoiding the censors, who, when it was published, threatened the author.[3] If there is no actual error, the True Fanatic invents one, just as Big Brother invented Immanuel Goldstein.

It should be added that, far and above domestic threats, the assailing of external foes by political fanatics will continue unabated. To take one example, having vilified the United States as the repository of all evil for the last forty years (and before), the megalomaniac gerontocrats who run the USSR can never be expected to admit that this is not so. All who expect such a thing will wait in vain. There is nothing the West or the United States could do to change this. It is a theological proposition, part of the ongoing *jihad* on the part of the Dictatorship of the Proletariat. All who expect an admission that Raoul Wallenberg, rescuer of hundreds of thousands of Jews during World War II, has been unjustly imprisoned or killed in the Soviet Union will wait in vain.

This is not to say that the Soviet Dictatorship of the Proletariat is composed of irrational people. But the fanatic need not be a wild-eyed, raving type like Khadafy. Kremlin bosses, however cool and diplomatic, are locked into their position by ideology. This is a kind of institutionalized, hereditary—even creedal—fanaticism. It can hardly be repeated enough that the True Fanatics—modern theocrats—see themselves not as mere rulers, world leaders, diplomats, or anything of the sort. No, they are the Incarnations of the Will of History, the Elect. As the Brezhnev doctrine has it, when a place like Afghanistan is changed by invaders from a backward authoritarian country into a more backward totalitarian one, this is called "passing into the next stage of history," of which they are "on the right side." Stationed in this lofty post one can well imagine that paranoia can indeed be a problem.

INVINCIBILITY

The one who believes himself infallible is likely to consider his hordes invincible as well. Equipped with such a belief, many a theocrat has had to learn the hard way, by meeting a ruinous and ignominious end. They remind one of the weasel described by Annie Dillard in *Teaching a Stone to Talk*. The creature locked onto the neck of an eagle and would not let go, even when pecked to death. When the eagle was shot, the hunter found the weasel's skull still attatched to the bird's throat by the jaws. Sometimes, in this manner, a True Fanatic's ambitions are his downfall. They are like a snake that swallows too large a prey and thus loses mobility and becomes an easy target. But they keep on trying to swallow.

Many a National Socialist thought the techniques of *blitzkrieg*, the superiority of the Aryan race, and the Great

Leader were a new trinity before whose power nothing could stand. But the Reich that was to prevail a thousand years did not last a generation. Blitzkrieg could be practiced by others; racial superiority is a falsehood; the great leader was much less than great.

Charles Manson, like all fanatics, was impatient. Denied the chance to use his songs to warn the world of a black uprising, he instituted plan B, which he considered an inexorable part of prophecy. He would get his followers to commit some horrible murders that he thought would be blamed on the blacks. The whites would then start a massive race war in retaliation, but lose out to the Black Muslims and Panthers. Much of the white race would be eliminated. Karma, Manson thought, dictated that it was the blacks' turn "to be on top." But unaccustomed to power, and being in Manson's view duller than people like himself, the blacks wouldn't know what to do, and in their distress would hand over the reigns of government to none other than, yes, Charles Manson, also known as God, aka Satan, who had been hiding in the bottomless pit in the desert. Conferred with power by the victorious blacks, he would then proceed to institute a society modeled on his infamous "family." He knew that it all just had to work.

With the advent of nuclear weapons, notions of invincibility become very dangerous indeed. This discussion need not be limited to what would happen if a Khadafy, Khomeini or Amin got their hands on a bomb. The world's premier theocracy, the USSR,[4] deploys many of these weapons and possesses a long-standing eschatology as well defined as that of Charles Manson: the Good Socialists (them) will vanquish the bad bourgeois democrats (USA, NATO); then, and only then, can the materialist millenium begin. Thus spake the prophets. The theoreticians in the Kremlin believe in the arrogant notion that they wield a mandate from History to turn the rest of the world into a dreary gulag like their own, after which the state will begin to wither away. Manson's wild schemes were no more ludicrous than these. Khrushchev's "We will bury you!" and Andrei Gromyko's threats to turn Italy into "another Pompei" are essentially the same thing as Charles Manson's dictum on the day of the Tate-La Bianca murders that, "Helter Skelter is coming down."

Khrushchev said that the USSR would not forget about Lenin "until shrimp learn to sing."[5] Lenin advocated the elimination of the enemy class, which in the current theocratic demonology means Western democracies. What a handy job for nuclear weapons! This is the only reason they are now likely to be used.

> Things become provocative in a productive sense only when *unilateral* disarmament is advocated. The trouble is that we should have no illusions about the Soviets. they would attempt to destroy us the minute they were reasonably sure they could win.[6]

This statement proceeds not from some general in NATO or the Pentagon, but from poet and folk singer Wolf Biermann. Booted out of East Germany in the seventies, Biermann is a high-profile member of the West German peace movement.

The True Fanatic, who wants to save/destroy/conquer the world, is the most dangerous creature alive; dangerous, too, in death. The Kremlin theocrats are in an awkward position. The prophecies are not only failing to come true, but are taking the opposite direction than that predicted by Marx. The lot of the Western worker has improved; the lot of the socialist worker has worsened. Western democracies attract people from all over the world; socialist theocracies shoot those who try to leave. Free, productive people export tons of food, even to their enemies; socialist theocracies cannot even feed themselves. (Although the ruling New Class eats well.) Socialist youth, who should be sparkling specimens of the New Man, will readily swap a leather-bound set of Marx and Lenin for a pair of Levis, a *Penthouse* magazine, or an Elton John album.

In short, the utopian Workers' Kingdom of Heaven on Earth is a failure by every standard. Those who cling to its superstitions and illusions can only be described as fanatics, however normal their demeanor. The last True Believers, (the most powerful True Fanatics in history), are in a difficult position. Being rational, they know that the game is up—that their socialist utopia is a squalid totalitarian fraud; but being infallible gods, custodians of the sacred mysteries of historical progress and dialectical materialism, they can never admit this. It just wouldn't look good. These men have the power to do away with the damning evidence—the West—in a matter of hours. If we allow them to be convinced of their invincibility, this may well happen. We can also pray that mass suicide for the glory of socialism will not be their Final Solution.

CHAPTER 4, NOTES
1. Vincent Bugliosi and Curt Gentry, *Helter Skelter* (New York: Norton, 1974), 246.
2. Ian Hunter, ed. *Things Past* (New York: Morrow, 1979), 35.
3. Malcolm Muggeridge, *Chronicles of Wasted Time* (New York: Morrow, 1973), 224.
4. The view of socialist dictators as theocrats was shared— perhaps originated— by George Orwell, who wrote in 1945, "A totalitarian state is in effect a theocracy, and its ruling cast, in order to keep its position, has to be thought of as infallible." See Orwell's essay "The Prevention of Literature" in *Inside the Whale and other Essays* (Middlesex: Penguin Books, 1962), 164.
5. Robert Payne, *The Life and Death of Lenin* (New York: Avon Books, 1964), VII.
6. From a lecture by Biermann at Cornell University. Quoted by Michael Greve in, "Greens Against the West," *National Review*, December 28, 1984, 25.

CHAPTER 5
I KILL,
THEREFORE I AM

Our examples of True Fanatics include: small people whose lack of stature nurtured an inferiority complex; people lacking in talent and competence who allowed hatred to fester, turning this very hatred into a ritual; men and women blindly devoted to a cause, animated by hopes of a utopia in which they would reign supreme; mere mortals who thought themselves infallible, rejecting all values and scruples; gods of stone, as serious as the statues on Easter Island, who seldom smiled and rarely laughed, except in triumph over a beaten enemy; and paranoiacs who saw enemies on every hand, real and imagined.

But above all, the True Fanatic joins all these characteristics of absolute idealism with absolute wickedness. The only result can be destruction and death on a massive scale.

Physician and philosopher Dr. Joseph-Ignace Guillotine set out to invent a machine that would be a quicker, less painful method of execution. It was entirely possible for a soldier wielding a sword to botch the job. He never imagined that his invention, inspired by machines of the Italian and German Renaissance, would facilitate mass executions. But in the hands of the Jacobins, it helped open a new era of mass murder.

This "holy guillotine," set up in the central square of cities and towns in the early 1790s, was put to work day and night, with people clamoring for more victims of the "national leveler." Death is perhaps the easiest path to *égalité*. The Jacobins made a ritual of these slayings, providing accompanying orchestras, holding up the severed heads to the cheers of the crowd. This sort of thing lead some to call the new ritual a "red mass" or "red theatre."[1]

The murderous Reign of Terror also provides what may be history's first examples of "liberation theologians." Certain priests sympathetic to the revolutionary regime exchanged the cross, the symbol of Christ's voluntary death, for the guillotine, an instrument for the forced liquidation of opponents. Just as Rev. Hewlett Johnson (that liberation theologian *par excellence* and patriarch of the movement) claimed that a mass murderer like Stalin was saving the world, these priests insisted that the guillotine, not the cross, would save the world. They wore miniature guillotines on chains around their necks, replacing crucifixes.[2] It appears that these gentle folk were ahead of their time in religious merchandising as well. Did they ever issue a pastoral letter on the merits of the decapitation of social enemies? It is not impossible.

In any case Dr. Guillotine could cure all ills. As the saying went, "I whisk off your head, and in a twinkling you have no pain!"

In the interests of economy where the guillotine was not available, enemies of the regime were blown up with cannon en masse. This was punishment by "national thunderbolt." The catalog of horrors is enormous, but why go on? This great Niagara of blood is not secular, nor even atheistic, but clearly pagan, right down to the religious trappings and nomenclature. Fanaticism as modern paganism will be dealt with later.

Above and beyond the mere fact of mass murder, one notices in the revolutionary executioners a total absence of guilt or remorse. They seem to perpetrate their deeds with nary a ripple of conscience. In similar style, Guatemalan revolutionary Mario Payeras describes the execution of an Indian youth who had asked to go home to his family. "When it was over, we were surprised to feel a sense of having matured."[3]

In some cases, there appears to be a clear, nearly sensual pleasure far beyond any imagined sense of justice. Revolutionary leaders like Fouche and Collot spoke of "hidden satisfactions" and "secret delights" in their tasks.[4] This too is a mark of a True Fanatic; he enjoys his work.

While there are many studies of the French Revolution, few such works exist about Stalin's reign of terror. Robert Conquest, in his book *The Great Terror*, estimates its victims at over ten million. Considering that not even some Soviet apologists, official and otherwise, deny these kind of numbers, it is quite likely that many more were, in fact, killed. One should add that most if not all of these victims were innocent of any charges against them.

Stalin, a prime example of a cold, calculating fanatic, derived great satisfaction from the death of others. Murder enabled him to emote and wax lyrical. In 1923 he remarked to Dzerzhinsky (a secret police official) and Kamenev: "To choose the victim, carefully prepare the blow, satisfy an implacable vengeance, then to bed . . . There is nothing sweeter in the world."[5] Dzherzhinsky, founder of what is now the KGB, doubtless had a few colorful stories of his own.

Both Lenin and Hitler considered mass liquidations of opponents as positively beneficial, laudable acts of social hygiene. They saw themselves as social surgeons removing a "bacillus" or "lice" from the scientific kingdom.

Mao Tse-tung faced the prospect of losing 300 million people in a war with a "so what."[6] He added that this would soon be forgotten and the Chinese could again get busy producing babies. An underachiever most of his life, he was doubtless proud of his purely political domestic liquidations.

It is hard to imagine Pol Pot killing some three million Cambodians out of a population of seven million without deriving some depraved personal pleasure from the slaughter. How is it possible that those who ordered such executions, whether in Cambodia, the USSR, Nazi Germany, or China, could not, after a time, revel in their task?

The Manson family killed innocent people not only in the belief that their acts would precipitate a black-white race war—a fulfillment of prophecy—but did so with a literally orgasmic joy. They followed the story of their own deeds on television. Manson bragged about the killings he had ordered or performed. "You have to have a real love in your heart to do this for people," explained murderer Susan Atkins.[7] More honestly, on another occasion, she described the murder of Sharon Tate as a "sexual release."[8]

This is obviously an example of human depravity at its nadir. It might be thought strictly criminal and its inclusion in this book mere sensationalism. But, on examination, is Susan Atkins delight in murder a whole lot different than Stalin's nearly poetic ode on the joys of assassination? I for one don't think so. It has long been recognized that there is a unity of truth, of goodness; but a unity of evil exists also. This theme should be worked out.

To the True Fanatic, who is everywhere on the march, acts of monstrous, barbaric cruelty are the commands of a super-personal force. He quashes impulses of mercy and kindness, since they appear to him as a kind of temptation. Such a creature will hence torment us endlessly. As Dostoevsky pointed out, he is, quite literally, possessed, bereft of humanity.

Carlos Marighella, author of *Mini Manual for Urban Guerrillas*, explains that "shooting and aiming are to the urban guerrilla what air and water are *to human beings*" (italics added).[9] The only clue that this sort of being is not completely sub-human is his occasional propensity to despair and suicide. And even in suicide, like the perverse Jim Jones, he sometimes tries to see how many he can take with him.

The True Fanatic, like the Gadarene swine, rushes resolutely downward to destruction. Lenin's nihilist mentor Sergey Nechayev, in the very first line of his *Catechism of a Revolutionary*, states that a person like himself "is a doomed man,"[10] but appears to relish this fact, confirming what was written long ago, that all who hate God and despise the divine wisdom "love death."[11]

CHAPTER 5, NOTES
1. Gérard de Puymège in *Fanaticism* (New York: Shocken Books, 1983), 106.
2. Ibid.
3. The description is from Payeras's *Los Dias de la Selva* ("Jungle Days") published in Cuba and unavailable (as yet) in English. It is reviewed and quoted by Mary Ball Martinez in "Implantations," *The American Spectator*, June 1985, 45.
4. Puymège, 110.
5. Cited by Malcolm Muggeridge, *Like it Was: The Diaries of Malcolm Muggeridge* (New York: Morrow, 1981), 378.
6. Paul Johnson, *Modern Times* (New York: Harper and Row, 1983), 546.
7. Vincent Bugliosi and Curt Gentry, *Helter Skelter* (New York: Norton, 1974), 85.
8. Ibid., 95.
9. Claire Sterling, *The Terror Network* (New York: Holt, Rinehart and Winston, 1981), 21.
10. Robert Payne, *The Life and Death of Lenin* (New York: Avon Books, 1964), 26.
11. Proverbs 8:36.

PART
2
THE FANATICAL FAITHFUL

CHAPTER 6
IN THE NAME
OF HEAVEN

BETWEEN INIQUITY AND INSINCERITY

There can be no doubt that True Fanatics have often been theocrats who do in fact perpetrate their deeds, as they imagine, in the service of God. Voltaire's description of fanaticism as "religion's rebel son" fits these above all others.

What André Gide said about nationalism, that it was wide of hatred and narrow of love, is also true of fanaticism among the religious. Although people of faith, one notices in every case that their demonology is stronger than that faith. Fanaticism of this type is no respecter of persons, religions, or denominations. The Protestant may point a finger at the Catholic persecutions of the Waldensians, which Pope Innocent VIII in his Bull of 1487 called, "so holy and necessary an extermination."[1] *Foxe's Book of Martyrs*, at one time half the average English Christian's library, chronicles many other atrocities committed by Catholics with fanatical zeal. But Luther's treatment of the Anabaptists and Calvin's incineration of Servetus should give the Protestant pause. And the Anabaptists themselves, as will be seen, boasted their own special brand of fanaticism. The Moslem may remind the Christian of the Crusades, but may himself be part of a contemporary *jihad*, a holy war, in which he earns paradise by killing innocent hostages or blowing "infidels" to tiny chunks in suicide bombing raids. Col. Khadafy declares:

> We have the right to take a legitimate and sacred action—an entire people liquidating its opponents inside and abroad in broad daylight.[2]

But from the Christian perspective, none of the various crusades, persecutions, or exterminations are episodes upon which the follower of Jesus Christ looks back in fondness.

It was for reasons like this that J.B.S. Haldane, an academic and communist polemicist with whom C.S. Lewis once crossed swords, proclaimed fanaticism a "Judeo-Christian invention." He thought it one of only four developments of great importance between 3000 B.C. and A.D. 1400.[3]

The secularist may consign all—Moslem holy warriors, crusading Calvinists, authoritarian Catholics, monastic flagellants, suicidal cultists—to his rubbish heap of contempt, forgetting (if he ever knew in the first place) that his brand of fanatic is every bit as religious and in nearly every case more extreme. The European religious wars are history; Pol Pot is news.

But even so, one must not neglect the fanatical faithful, although, due to the abundance of material already in existence, the treatment will be brief. The Spanish Inquisition is a classic example.

By an accident of lexicography, "inquisition" falls somewhere between iniquity and insincerity, concepts it very much embodies. Somehow the medieval church imagined itself as the scourge of God whose task was to purge Christendom of all evil. One can scour the New Testament for commandments to do this sort of thing. God insists that vengeance belongs to him (Hebrews 10:30). The parables of Jesus indicate the coexistence of good and evil until the end, when God himself will separate them. But the popes and priests of the time saw things differently. Men have never been bashful about usurping God's prerogative of judgment. And, in any case, the New Testament was not then the supreme authority to the Roman Church.

It is no surprise that in a place like medieval Spain demonology should be stronger than faith. Any time the Church enjoys a monopoly not only of ecclesiastical but secular power, one finds a great weakening of spirituality. One's religion can easily become a matter of heredity, nationalism, and pageantry. Some notable exceptions to this rule—that is, people of genuine spirituality—found themselves under suspicion in Spain.

Fray Luis de Leon taught at the University of Salamanca and was considered one of Spain's greatest scholars and poets. He got in trouble with the theologians of the Inquisition for regarding the Hebrew text of the Old Testament as more authoritative than the Latin Vulgate. (The fact that he was a converted Jew was also of interest to the inquisitors.) Arrested and imprisoned for four and a half years, he returned to his university post and began his lecture: "*Como dijimos ayer*"—"as we said yesterday." Asked by a student why he spoke so softly, he replied "so the gentlemen of the Inquisition will not hear." It turned out that they did hear, and he was very nearly arrested again.

The period of the Inquisition also saw the rise of the visionary reformer Santa Teresa de Avila, and the artist Velásquez. It should be mentioned as well that it was during the noontide of inquisitional abuses that a one-armed writer named Miguel de Cervantes wrote *Don Quijote*, one of the greatest novels of all time. Although the Church censored tiny parts of it, the book was freely published and read. It still is.

Though a host of exaggerations have surrounded the Inquisition, there can be no doubt of its brutalities and crimes. In the name of God, priests would stretch the accused on a rack, pour water down their throats, and myriad other tortures. Property was confiscated upon accusation, fabulously enriching the church. Bodies were exhumed and burned, the biblical text John 15:6 being used as justification. ("If a man does not abide in me, he is cast forth as a branch and withers; and the branches are gathered, thrown into the fire and burned.") The *auto de fe*,[4] Spanish for "act of faith," consisting of public burnings, was a common spectacle with the atmosphere of a country fair.

Oxford historian Cecil Roth has pointed out that the Inquisition was in fact a tribunal,[5] and that the inquisitors generally went after only those against whom they thought they had an airtight case. There was nothing of the wholesale slaughter of friend and foe as under Stalin, Mao, and especially Pol Pot. Jews who had converted to a nominal Christianity under duress, but who persisted in Jewish customs, were the main targets. Catholic heretics, Moslems, and Protestants (domestic and foreign) also numbered among the victims. Although the sincerity of the inquisitors may well be doubted, their official object was to either convert or restore such ones to the fold of the Church. Far from going after only their enemies, modern True Fanatics like Lenin advocate wholesale extermination: a person's "class," his birth, his background, mark him for destruction with no hope of salvation. There is no Pope or God to appeal to, as there was in the Inquisition.[6] Furthermore, the modern True Fanatic cannot tolerate a Cervantes or Velásquez, as the Spanish inquisitors could.

With Spain being such a Catholic monolith with nothing to fear from judaizing Christians, why then were they persecuted so fiercely? Here a True Fanatic comes into play.

Torquemada, the first Grand Inquisitor, was described as exceptionally intolerant even for his time. Was this intolerance entirely the result of religious zeal? Perhaps, but how interesting to discover that Torquemada was part Jewish himself.

In like manner, rumor had it that Charles Manson's father was black, hence Manson's hatred of blacks. Some writers have speculated that Hitler was part Jewish, explaining his fury against Jews in a state dedicated to an Aryan master race.[7] The latter case closely parallels that of Torquemada. This kind of personal animosity against an ethnic group probably has as much to do with the ferocity of the Inquisition as any desire for theological purity.

Torquemada lived in regal style, bloated with wealth confiscated from his victims. Though surrounded by guards and soldiers, he lived in constant fear of assassination. His record of cruelty, persecution, and torture is a reminder of what has been done in the name of heaven, but partly to justify one's own passions.

CHAPTER 6, NOTES
  1. Gérard de Puymège, *Fanaticism* (New York: Shocken Books, 1983), 211.
  2. "Libya Declares Right to Kill Opponents No Matter Where," *Philadelphia Enquirer*, 3 March 1985.
  3. J.B.S. Haldane, *The Inequality of Man* (New York; Famous Books, 1938), 49.
  4. The more common form is the Portuguese auto da fé.
  5. Cecil Roth, *The Spanish Inquisition* (New York: Norton, 1964), VII.
  6. Ibid., 60.
  7. See Eugene H. Methvin, "Hitler and Stalin, Twentieth Century Superkillers," *National Review*, 31 May 1985, 25.

CHAPTER 7
IN THE NAME
OF THE MILLENIUM

Fanatical persecutions in the name of heaven may well be outstripped by fanaticism in the name of a millenium. The two are not the same. Thomas Muntzer, venerated by radical Anabaptists and modern Marxists as an early class warrior, is a shining example.

Far from being the downtrodden peasant of Marxist legend, Muntzer grew up in relative comfort and spent a large part of his life in school, to the point that some have called him an eternal student, a species common in our day. He cannot have had a great deal of practical experience, something any aspiring fanatic does well to avoid. Like Lenin, Muntzer seems to have been steeped in the theoretical. Though he possessed enormous erudition in the Scriptures, theology, and philosophy, his learning seems to have been an attempt to solve a personal problem, a problem of faith. Though ordained a priest, Muntzer struggled about the truth of Christianity, and even about the existence of God. He wandered about, restless, in search of certainty. What "fulfilled" him, it turned out, was not a more robust faith, or a busy preaching ministry, but rather a clearly defined demonology.

Encouraged by Luther's attacks on the Papacy, Muntzer broke with Catholicism. But he was soon to break with Luther as well, and wound up identifying the German reformer with the Whore of Babylon in the book of Revelation.

The teaching that most appealed to Muntzer was not Luther's justification by faith alone; this was too personal and quietistic. What stirred Muntzer's juices was a regurgitation of the millenarian Taborite doctrine in which the Elect would annihilate the godless. On Muntzer's prophetic chart, this holy war of bloody extermination had to take place before Christ could come and the Millenium began. The homicide taboo was not a difficult hurdle for Muntzer, of whom Norman Cohn noted:

> Abandoning Luther, he now thought and talked only of the Book of Revelation and of such incidents in the Old Testament as Elijah's slaughter of the priests of Baal, Jehu's slaying of the son's of Ahab and Jael's assassination of the sleeping Sisera. Contemporaries noted and lamented the change that had come over him, the lust for blood which at times expressed itself in sheer raving.[1]

From the one extreme of the secluded, scholarly man of ideas and unsettled mysticism, he shot like a comet to the opposite pole of a radical demagogue and violent man of action. For him there could be no middle ground.

But above all, Muntzer fits the description of the True Fanatic: one who by his own agency undertakes the Sisyphus task of bringing in Paradise, a Kingdom of Heaven on Earth. This sets him in contrast to Luther, in whose eschatology God was the agent of judgment. Luther's concept of the Kingdom of Heaven was also transcendent, not earthly. In Luther's view, Rome would be overcome not by arms, but by the preaching of the gospel. In order to preach the gospel a stable social order was needed, hence Luther eschewed social upheaval and revolt. This earned him Muntzer's everlasting enmity.

Students of Muntzer's writings have noted that he said very little about what actual conditions in the Millenium would be like. But about the mass extermination needed to launch the Millenium he had plenty of information. In this he resembles Karl Marx, who declared that those who speculated about what everyone would do after the revolution were "reactionaries." Marx's writings also abound in dark, violent forebodings. To repeat an earlier principle of fanaticism: demolition and extermination come before construction.

Muntzer also resembles Marx in that he did little, if anything, to improve the conditions of the peasants among whom he lived. In fact, he sometimes told his followers to obey their masters' most exorbitant demands. Perhaps it was because the conditions of the peasantry were improving at the time, and because some of the princes opposed by Muntzer were generous, tolerant men.

But the fanatic is neither satisfied with himself nor with any earthly conditions, nor, by and large, with people. They all must be changed. The god of the fanatic is not the omnipotent God of the Bible but in fact an idol, a dependent creature who cannot bring judgment alone; he must have human help.

Theologically, Muntzer made a practical distinction between the historical Jesus and the "inner Christ"—his version of the Holy Spirit. This was, ultimately, his convoluted way of saying that he himself had become God, something he did in fact claim.[2] The notion of invincibility is a logical follow-up to this. As he imagined, Muntzer would be able to dodge the cannonballs of the enemy, or even catch them in his clothing. Like some modern utopians and believers in a phantom Age of Aquarius, Muntzer adopted the rainbow as a symbol and placed it on his banner. Apparently during one fiery speech, a real rainbow appeared in the sky. This appeared to be a signal of a sure victory that, like the promised kingdom, never came.

Muntzer's role in the Peasant's Revolt has been the subject of much debate, and this book is no place to launch into a full treatment of that upheaval which had multiple causes and effects like any other conflict. In any case, during one battle Muntzer did not try to catch cannonballs in his clothing and fling them back at the troops of the Whore of Babylon. Rather, he and just about everyone else fled in panic. But by the time of this sudden splashdown into reality, it was too late for change. This is frequently the way fanatics meet their end.

The armies of the princes destroyed the opposition and found Muntzer hiding in a cellar in Frankenhausen. He was tortured and then beheaded. The Man Who Would Be God had impaled himself on the flaming sword barring the way to the earthly paradise. In spite of his mystical megalomania couched in Christian terms, he remains a prototype to modern, secular fanatics better prepared, better armed, but still laboring under three superstitions: that man is perfectible; that an earthly paradise can be established by men; and that those who are ushering in this paradise have the right to dispose of those who stand in their way.

CHAPTER 7, NOTES

1. Norman Cohn, *The Pursuit of the Millenium: Revolutionary Millenarians and Mystical Anarchists of the Middle Ages* (New York: Oxford, 1970), 236.
2. Ibid.

CHAPTER 8
IN THE NAME OF THE MILLENIUM, CONTINUED

A EUROPEAN GUYANA

In the current state of things, a writer of satire—or even horror or fantasy—sets a difficult task for himself. Reality, as novelist Philip Roth has noted, is often more far-fetched that anything a scribe can invent.

To cite one example, Malcolm Muggeridge once attended a performance of the musical *Godspell*. As the show closed, a prominent Church of England clergyman bolted to his feet and shouted, "Long live God!" Mr. Muggeridge, who counts buffoonish clergymen among his favorite bull's-eyes, confessed that a satirist such as himself is "broken and defeated" by such incidents. All he could do in his description of the event was suggest some alternate lines for the Reverend, such as "Carry on eternity!" or "Hang in there, infinity!" Neither matches the original for sheer, unintended comedy.

In a more serious vein, imagine some pulp novelist or producer of cheap horror films dishing up a tale along the lines of Reverend Jim Jones's mass suicide in Guyana. A warm reception for such a thing, whether by the audience or by critics, would not be likely, partly because suicide "doesn't play" as well as, say, murder or bombing. And hundreds of blacks following a white minister into the jungle? As fiction, it just wouldn't work.

But unbelievable atrocities did emerge, not from the steaming vaults of fantasy, but out of the hard quarry of history and fact. Although the mass suicide at Jonestown was unparalleled, there have been other colonies similar to Jonestown in earlier times. It is dubious that Jones knew about them, for if he did, his own colony might have seen even more fanatical excesses. As it stands, the communal efforts of two radical protestants reveal striking parallels to Jonestown.

It all took place in 1534 in the German city of Munster, a community of some fifteen thousand people. Although Roman Catholics lived there, it was officially designated a Lutheran town. However, followers of the militant Anabaptist Melchior Hoffman were at the time being banished from other areas and streaming into the place. They came to dominate much of town life, especially among the poorer classes. Even Bernt Rothmann, a prominent Lutheran preacher, converted to Anabaptism and began preaching a form of anarchism-communism based on the early chapters of the book of Acts and the Fourth Epistle of Clement, which even non-Christian scholars regard as spurious.

While Melchior Hoffman was a man of peace who eschewed violence and counseled patient waiting for God to bring in the millennium Himself, some of his followers in Munster were of a different outlook.

They were, in fact, not from Munster at all, but foreigners from Holland where Anabaptists were being persecuted in the wake of a failed uprising. Two of these, John Matthys and John Bockelson, were militants considered by their followers to be Enoch and Elijah, the two "witnesses" of the book of Revelation. They believed that people such as themselves needed to take up the sword against those who would not receive their message. The ungodly, in their view, had no right to live. As the numbers of such people dramatically increased, the burghers of the town grew alarmed, but a swell of religious enthusiasm swept over the general populace. There were over a thousand rebaptisms within a week's time.

The would-be Enoch and Elijah ran through the streets urging people to repent of their sins. An outbreak of hysteria followed. Some of the recent converts, particularly converted nuns, reported seeing apocalyptic visions. Others writhed on the ground, foaming at the mouth. Matthys and Bockelson took advantage of the wave of prophetic sentiment and, along with followers, occupied the Town Hall. They prevailed because the Lutherans, though still a majority, were unwilling to use the armed force made available by the Bishop. In addition, some members of the city council sympathized with the Anabaptists. Rather than take any action, many Lutherans and Catholics simply left town. Leading Anabaptists urged their co-religionists from other areas to move to Munster. Like Jones's Guyana colony, Munster was portrayed as a city of refuge from the impending wrath of God, a new Jerusalem. With a comfortable majority, the Anabaptists dominated the next elections for city council. But though they attained power by semi-democratic means, their regime was a pure communist theocracy. G.H. Williams comments:

> Politically supervised communism in Munster may be said to have been an outgrowth of military exigency reinforcing a desire inherent in Anabaptism everywhere to restore the communal life of the primitive church as recorded in Acts and the Pseudo Clementine Epistle IV.[1]

Wasting little time, the new theocrats began to loot churches and monasteries, burning and banning all books but the Bible. This theocratic revolution, like all others, was stridently anti-intellectual, anti-scholastic, and anti-aesthetic. Other reformers, like Luther and Zwingli, were men of immense erudition and even artistic skill; not so with the self-proclaimed Enoch and Elijah. Where Luther debated and appealed to the Scriptures, they denounced and appealed to their own inspiration. This pair more resembles

Jim Jones, who saw himself as a reincarnation of Christ and Lenin (with Lenin enjoying a distinct advantage).

We have said there can be no dissent in a theocracy. How can a man who sees himself as the usher of the millennium, surrounded by adoring followers, tolerate dissent? Moreover, this theocracy would have to be purged of all evil and uncleanness as soon as possible. Matthys wanted to execute those Lutherans and Catholics who remained in the city, but finally settled for expulsion. In bitter, February cold, Matthys, along with armed bands, drove the unwanted from the city; young and old, infants and handicapped, pregnant women. The Anabaptists mocked and beat them as they left, robbing them of all their possessions and even of the food they carried. "Get out, you godless ones!" was the cry, "you enemies of the Father!"[2]

The evil ones now being purged, any divergence from the orthodoxy of John Matthys became punishable by death. The proof-text cited for this was Amos 9:10: "All the sinners of my people shall die by the sword."

The fanaticism of Matthys and Bockelson in implementing this egalitarian, communist theocracy is nowhere better demonstrated than in their rule against closing doors on houses, even at night! This was during the month of March, when it was still cold. They did, however, show great compassion by allowing a kind of screen or grate to keep out pigs and chickens.

Munster fell under siege about this time, but the weakness of the Bishop's troops and the solidarity of the Munster communards prevented the city's fall. These Anabaptists bore little resemblance to their Swiss and Southern German brethren who believed in the separation of church and state. Likewise, they diverge greatly from current Anabaptist pacifists such as Mennonites. In Munster, everyone was conscripted for some militarily-related duty: even young children were taught to shoot.[3]

Meanwhile, within the walls, Matthys's Anabaptist politburo doled out food and provisions confiscated from the expelled "enemies." Rothmann and his fellow preachers had become the regime's propagandists, railing against the private use of money. [4] Besides rebaptism, Norman Cohn notes that the surrender of money was made a test of one's faith. [5] It was held to be evil, but instead of destroying it, citizens were urged to hand it over to the leaders. Jim Jones also practiced such larceny. Furthermore, with this kind of ideology long advocated by Hoffman and others, it cannot be contended that confiscation of goods was entirely a response to the Bishop's military siege. Rothmann, demonstrating a true, fanatical utopianism, envisioned a future (but earthly) state of affairs in which work itself would be unnecessary. But as it stood, he believed that, under Matthys and Bockelson, "community" had been restored.

Then, as now, the True Fanatics boasted admirers and apologists. Contemporary examples are Western support for Mao, and even for the late Enver Hoxha of Albania. During Matthys's reign, the farther away such admirers lived the more ebullient their hopes that Munster did, in fact, represent the dawn of the Messianic Age. Those who lived nearby knew better.

As Bernard-Henri Lévy has perceptively written, collectivism is impossible without terror, and terror soon began in Munster. The City Council now amounted to nothing more than a squad of toadies and sycophants for John Matthys. Things did not fare well with those who were less than worshipful of the foreigner who was dispersing their goods.

Hubert Reuscher, a blacksmith and native of the town, apparently called Matthys a deceiver in public. A kangaroo court (the only kind that exists in theocracies) hastily assembled in the main square and Reuscher was denounced. The few citizens who questioned the legality of the "trial" were imprisoned. Following this, Matthys personally stabbed and shot Reuscher. This incident and others like it struck such terror into the hearts of the populace that Matthys was able to hold sway with little difficulty. In Munster, he was god and Bockelson was assistant god. Under their auspices, fanatical collectivism continued.

Like Thomas Muntzer and a host of other True Fanatics, Matthys began to feel invincible. Convinced that a small band led by himself could vanquish the besieging armies, he set forth to mop them up personally. As it happened, he and his party were mercilessly slaughtered. But if there was any rejoicing in Munster over the death of this tyrant, it was short-lived. First John had died; Second John quickly took over.

John Bockelson (also known as John of Leiden) boasted the finest fanatical credentials. Like Charles Manson he was, literally, a bastard. Like Hitler he was a poor student with just enough learning to make him dangerous. Where Lenin failed as a lawyer, Bockelson proved a commercial disaster as a tailor. He also aspired to be a theater impresario, playwright, and actor, but cannot have been too successful at this other than learning how to perform for a crowd, something that was to serve him well. There can be no doubt that the militant Anabaptist millenarianism proved a collective entity in which he could submerge himself and in which his failures would be swallowed up. But his gifts and appearance were such that, coupled with the state of terror instituted by Matthys, Bockelson could rule a city of 15,000 people through times of hardship and attack for more than a year. This was a man in his mid-twenties. The fanatic is often able to cast an effective spell, with or without the choreographed spectacle favored by modern totalitarians. The denizens of Munster resembled the journalists who tried to see the good side of Jim Jones. Without their cooperation, Bockelson could have done nothing.

So abject was their veneration that when Bockelson charged about naked through the streets like a Doukhobor,[6] and then fell into a trance for several days, no one considered deposing him. It was a terrible mistake. And if this were not bad enough, when Bockelson snapped out of his trance his "revelations" were accepted without question!

The visionary then dissolved the council and ruled the town himself, along with twelve appointed elders on the Old Testament model. He not only retained Matthys's collectivist practices, but made them stricter. Artisans were to work for no compensation. The death penalty was applied to offences as trivial as quarreling. Just how many executions for minor offences were carried out is not clear, but there surely were some. One can't be too careful wielding the sword in the kingdom. But Bockelson was just starting to hit stride.

He not only began to practice polygamy, acquiring fifteen wives, but made polygamy a law. All women under a certain age were required to marry. Resistance to the law meant death, and some women were in fact executed. The multiplicity of wives caused such chaos and strife that Bockelson finally allowed divorce, and eventually dispensed with the marriage ceremony altogether. One can only imagine what went on under these conditions, but it must have been close to a massive sexual orgy. Men competed to see who could acquire the most wives. The preacher Rothmann boasted nine. (Why, one wonders, did he not stop at the biblical number of seven, or push on to twelve?) The state of affairs in which people would not have to work had probably arrived for him. In a statement that will not endear him to feminists, he defended polygamy by saying that, if a man is dependent on one wife, "she leads him about like a bear on a rope."[7]

One of Bockelson's harem of fifteen apparently got too uppity and paid for it dearly. In the market square, in full view of the public, Bockelson personally beheaded her, then wildly stomped on her dead body.[8] The other girls probably stayed in line after this. Not even Jim Jones, who engaged in sex with many of his followers (male and female) and forced dissenters to commit acts of depravity in view of everyone, can match this Anabaptist.

Some who opposed polygamy attempted to overthrow Bockelson's theocracy, and even managed to toss the man and some of his cohorts into prison. But the rebels did not prevail and some fifty people were killed in reprisals. Two mercenaries who had defected from the besieging armies were shot for creating a disturbance in a tavern.

While all this bizarre social and sexual behavior was taking place, the communards somehow managed to remain a disciplined fighting force against the Bishop's troops. They not only ferociously repelled attacks, but succeeded in sneaking out and sabotaging enemy guns. They even managed to persuade over a hundred troops to defect! Did they entice the weary, underpaid soldiers of the Bishop with tales of polygamous adventures and the promise of ecstasy? It is not impossible. Like all True Fanatics, Bockelson, in spite of his mystical tendencies, did have a shrewd, pragmatic dimension. Similarly, Eastern Bloc spies now offer big money, not socialist visions and stirring speeches, to those who would sell out their countries.

Bockelson might have vanquished the Bishop's armies entirely and even pushed on to take other cities, but like First John he succumbed to his own delusions. After one resounding military victory, when the besiegers were totally demoralized and even in a state of desertion, Bockelson, rather than press his advantage, had himself proclaimed king—the "Messiah of the Last Days."

In short order Bockelson was decked out in the most ridiculous excesses of megalomaniacal splendor that would have made other True Fanatics throughout history pass out with joy. The craftsmen of the town fitted him with flowing robes and gold ornaments. He held forth in a luxurious court of some two hundred people and had a throne set up in the marketplace. Here he would arrive, mounted and crowned, to rule his subjects. The emblem of his new state was a globe pierced with swords, topped by a cross inscribed, "One king of righteousness over all."[9] Imagine the new, positive self-image of the half-baked tailor and thespian. So much of history is a tale of True Fanatics getting what they want. Bockelson surely had it all.

But by 1535 the Bishop's reinforced blockade was taking its toll. By April of that year, famine conditions prevailed everywhere but the royal court. People were forced to eat rats and mice. Instances of cannibalism were reported. Bockelson diverted the populace by staging various spectacles such as dancing, plays, and athletic contests. Like Jones, he tested their loyalty by summoning them to what would have surely been a suicidal military sortie against the enemy, only to turn the event into a huge banquet, an *auto de fe*, at which a captured soldier was beheaded.

By June, daily executions for such crimes as attempted desertion were commonplace and usually carried out by the New Messiah who, far from showing any reluctance, proclaimed that he would gladly kill all priests, monks, and kings. Like all True Fanatics, this one enjoyed his work. He sometimes ordered bodies dismembered and posted in public places as a warning.

Bockelson surely would have preferred that the whole town starve to death rather than surrender. It is distinctly possible that he could have staged his own "mass suicide for the glory of socialism," or even personally killed off most of the populace. But it was not to be. This earthly paradise, like all others, was built on sand.

Hans Eck and Henry Gresbeck, two men of the town, stole away by night and revealed a weakness in the fortifications to the enemy troops. In a surprise night attack on June 24, 1535, the Bishop's troops entered the town and displayed their own brand of fanaticism. They offered safe conduct to the few Anabaptists who had not already been slaughtered but, when they surrendered, went ahead and killed most of them anyway.

At the behest of the Bishop, the Messiah of the Last Days, aka Enoch and King of Righteousness, was led about in public like a circus animal. He maintained, however, that he had always sought God's glory. This can be believed since he really worshiped himself. He was finally tortured to death. The iron cage in which his mutilated body was publicly displayed may be seen in Munster today.

There were other fanatically homicidal Anabaptists at the time, who, like Bockelson and Muntzer, met a ruinous end. Though they are not typical of Anabaptism, much less of Protestantism, they show that the superstition of a collectivist kingdom of heaven on earth brought in by mortal men can lead to fanaticism of the worst kind. Let Ronald Knox supply an epitaph:

> Not less obstinately did the garrison of Munster lift up their eyes in expectation to heavens which should have been rent, and remained dumb. [10]

CHAPTER 8, NOTES

1. G.H. Williams, The Radical Reformation (Philadelphia: Westminster, 1962), 370.
2. Norman Cohn, The Pursuit of the Millennium (New York: Oxford, 1970), 262.
3. Williams, 370.
4. Modern radical Christians hold similar positions sometimes urging others to "throw their money in a ditch if they can't give it away." See Ann Munroe, "Devout Dissidents," The Wall Street Journal, 24 May 1985, 10.
5. Cohn, 265.
6. The Doukhobors are a Russian non-conformist sect that emigrated to Canada early in this century. They protest government policy by taking off their clothes. Early Quakers also "went naked for a sign." A group of early Anabaptists in Amsterdam ran naked through the streets and refused to dress when brought before the magistrates. "We are the naked truth," they said. See Ronald Knox, Enthusiasm (New York: Oxford, 1959), 136.
7. Williams, 378.
8. Ibid., 380.
9. Cohn, 272.
10. Knox, 137.

PART
3
THE FANATIC
IN FICTION

CHAPTER 9
THE FANATIC IN FICTION

Given the rule that instances of fanaticism in reality so often outstrip anything one can invent, is prying into the world of fiction on this subject worth the trouble? Once production-line, "religious fanatic" caricatures like Elmer Gantry have been discarded, the answer is a resounding yes. Good fiction can crystallize a character, a time in history, a mania, as nothing else can. Listen to Frederic Rene de Sainte Claude, a revolutionary in Durrenmatt's play *The Marriage of Mr. Mississippi*:

> There is only justice without God. Nothing can help man but man. . . . Man cannot keep God's law, he has to create his own law. We have both shed blood; you have slain three hundred and fifty criminals, I have never counted my victims. What we are doing is murder, therefore we must do it to some purpose. You have acted in the name of God, I in the name of Communism. My deed is better than yours, for I am seeking something in time, while you are seeking something in eternity. What the world needs is not redemption from sin but redemption from hunger and oppression. [1]

Solzhenitsyn's *One Day in the Life of Ivan Denisovich* conveys the reality of the gulag better than any sociological study. (None have been written by impartial observers in any case.) George Orwell's *Homage to Catalonia* preserves some neglected truths about the Spanish Civil War in contrast to the serpentine edifice of lies that has arisen around that conflict. Malcolm Muggeridge's *Winter in Moscow* is a more compelling and accurate portrait of Soviet life in the thirties than the slavishly apologetic "news" articles of Walter Duranty for the *New York Times*. On this dimension of fiction Muggeridge explains:

> The imagination, at however rudimentary a level, reaches into the future. So its works have a prophetic quality. A Dostoevsky foresees just what a revolution will mean in Russia—in a sense, foresees the Soviet regime and Stalin; whereas a historian like Miliukov and his liberal-intellectual friends envisage the coming of an amiable parliamentary democracy.[2]

It hardly needs mentioning who was right.

Surveying the literary and cultural output of Russians in the last century, one could say that their achievements were unparalleled, particularly in music and fiction. What a cultural force these people would be today if their creative capacities were not gagged and bound in the maximum-security dungeon of Stalinist censorship. These people *think*, and when they think they write. E.M. Forster, author of *A Passage to India*, admitted that no English novelist had explored man's soul like Dostoyevsky.[3] Some of the great works of English literature Forster considered as mere cottages beside the mighty colonnades of *War and Peace* and *The Brothers Karamazov*. Scottish author Thomas Carlyle wondered how people imagined they could write if they first did not see and believe. Dostoyevsky did both, and was able to write much of great enduring value. But first a look at another Russian writer.

CHAPTER 9, NOTES

1. Friedrich Durrenmatt, *The Marriage of Mr. Mississippi, in Four Plays*, trans. Gerhard Nellhaus (London: Jonathan Cape, 1964), 159.
2. Malcolm Muggeridge, *Chronicles of Wasted Time* (New York: Morrow, 1973), 14.
3. E.M. Forster, *Aspects of the Novel* (New York: Harcourt, Brace and World, 1927), 7.

CHAPTER 10
THE MAN WHO KNEW EVERYTHING

A man must be a savage.
Bazarov, from *Fathers and Sons*

Ivan Turgenev's *Fathers and Sons* (1861) created a storm of controversy for its portrayal of the nihilist Eugeny Vassilyev Bazarov. Russian youth chided Turgenev for caricaturing their heroes, while the older generation thought the author was not clear just where he stood personally vis-à-vis his protagonist's nihilism. In any case, Turgenev presents a subject so finely drawn as to suggest portraiture, or even disguised autobiography, although the former is surely the case.

Fathers and Sons begins with the return of Bazarov and his friend Arkady Kirsanov from university, where Bazarov is a medical student. They first stay at the Kirsanov estate, where Bazarov flaunts his nihilist ideas before the old folks, baiting them into philosophical jousts.

Nihilists of Turgenev's day, like their spiritual descendants, took the position of being champions of the poor. We are told that Bazarov "possessed the special faculty for inspiring confidence in people of a lower class." One notices, though, that Bazarov also regularly insults the servants. It seems that his advocacy of their cause bears no relation to his own affections, nor to his social position. Certainly neither Bazarov nor Arkady Kirsanov are themselves poor.

Arkady's father, Nikolai, was a liberal of sorts, already in the process of dividing up his estate among the serfs. For this he had been called a "Red" by some of the neighbors. Bazarov's father was a retired doctor, not a man of great wealth but not a plebeian either. Like Arkady he had been treated with genuine love, even fawned over all his life in spite of his provocative, radical views. But often in conversation Bazarov drops descriptions of the older generation like, "Trash. Rotten little aristocrats,"[1] leaving no doubt that this applies across the board. The reforms of landowners like Nikolai amounted, in Bazarov's view, to erecting a building on a condemned site. None of this mattered. The older set had had their day.

This is remarkably consistent with the fanatical mindset that fails to find satisfaction in any reform, any good intention, any practical expression of concern. On this point he is insatiable, and Turgenev's character exemplifies this perfectly.

At school, Bazarov has turned Arkady into something of a convert to nihilism although it is apparent that he is still learning, albeit without great enthusiasm. Arkady announces to his parents that his guest, "knows everything,"[2] something that Bazarov would not be bashful about claiming for himself as a representative of new Scientific Man. Like Lenin, Bazarov is an adroit arguer who can dish out abuse with great skill. He is a class warrior who comes to rumble. Though a competent medical student, Bazarov, like archfanatic Nechayev, is most occupied with the science of destruction. He challenges opponents to cite "a single institution in our present mode of life, in family or social life, that does not call for complete and unqualified repudiation."[3] This is the weltanschauung of the nihilist: a preoccupation with negation, repudiation, destruction. It is rhetoric over reason, demonology over faith, demolition over construction. Everything else flows from this.

An unabashed empiricist, Bazarov has no use for

metaphysics. As he returns from capturing frogs for dissection, Pavel, Arkady's uncle, remarks that this young student, "has no faith in principles, but he has faith in frogs."[4] This just about summed the matter up. Even Arkady is shocked when his mentor remarks that a certain woman's body is, "perfect for the dissecting table."[5] This was undoubtedly a joke, but the nihilist's jokes, like his dreams, have a way of coming true.

During one spirited debate, Nikolai Kirsanov tells Bazarov, "You deny everything; or, speaking more precisely, you destroy everything. But one must construct too."

"That is not our business now," Bazarov replies, "The ground has to be cleared first."[6]

Since Turgenev penned these perceptive lines, a lot of ground-clearing has taken place. Much of the leveled territory has been used for the graves of the innocent.

Bazarov not only displays scant creative aptitude (except for creatively carving up frogs), but actively despises art. "A good chemist is twenty times as useful as any poet,"[7] he says, adding on another occasion that "Raphael's not worth a brass farthing."[8] He think it ludicrous that Arkady's father plays the cello and spends time reading Pushkin. When it comes to culture, the fanatic reaches for his Smith and Wesson.

Not that Bazarov is a "flat" character failing to display normal human ambivalence. He blushes when meeting the story's heroine and love interest, Odintsova, but we learn that he considers romantic love a kind of disease. "A man hasn't time to attend to such trifles; a man must be savage,"[9] he comments.

Fathers and Sons is thin on story; the characterization of the central figure is its major strength. Bazarov is placed in various situations that will best elucidate all dimensions of his philosophy, if nihilism can be called a philosophy. There is an episodic quality to the tale; one thing does not necessarily lead to another. Therefore, when Bazarov contracts typhus after performing an autopsy and promptly dies, one is tempted to agree with Forster that this novelist, like many others, is using death as a neat sort of cop-out because he could not think of another way to end the story. But whether this is true or not, it goes without saying that artistically Turgenev is superb. Bazarov's deathbed scene is surely one of the most moving passages in all of literature. And if the ending does not work structurally, it certainly fits thematically. There is always a sense of the tragic around people like Bazarov.

Fanatics, allowed to follow their premises, frequently do so with disastrous results for everyone. Had he lived on, Bazarov might well have wound up dissecting people like a mad, Russian Dr. Mengele, or something roughly equivalent. After all, he told everyone who would listen that, "the ground had to be cleared." Certainly Bazarov's historical counterpart, the Bolsheviks, thought little of sweeping away, "Trash. Rotten little aristocrats."

Perhaps Turgenev found it necessary to destroy his character in order to save him, because death saved Bazarov from his own hateful self. Quite often this is what it takes. The specimen of New Scientific Man, who recognized no authority but thought himself capable of establishing a new, more just order, is a changed person when he mounts the coal-black stallion of death. He seems for the first time to experience genuine human feelings of love. He sees his failures and admits that people like himself are "not needed"[10] in Russia. No, windy, half-baked students are not the backbone of any social order. It is the shoemaker, the tailor, and other common, normal[11] types that he has for so long despised and insulted that are needed. Turgenev ends the tale on a note of hope—the possibility of eternal reconciliation and life without end. The fanatic is not beyond redemption. The great Russian writer knew that death ends hatred but magnifies love.

CHAPTER 10, NOTES

1. Ivan Turgenev, *Fathers and Sons*, trans. Ralph Matlaw, (New York: Norton, 1966), 37.
2. Ibid., 6.
3. Ibid., 42.
4. Ibid., 18.
5. Ibid., 62.
6. Ibid., 39.
7. Ibid., 19.
8. Ibid., 42.
9. Ibid., 88.
10. Ibid., 161.
11. The contempt for the common, normal life seems to have been picked up wholesale by modern radical clerics. Daniel Berrigan, for example, speaks of those "afflicted with the wasting disease of normalcy," who "reach out with an instinctive spasm in the direction of their loved ones," instead of participating in the peace movement with acceptable levels of zeal. The passage is quoted, favorably, in Ron Sider's *Nuclear Holocaust and Christian Hope* (Downer's Grove: InterVarsity Press, 1983), 291.

CHAPTER 11
THE POSSESSED

When the Dictatorship of the Proletariat of the USSR dubs a novel, "socially obnoxious and detrimental to the cause of socialism," one may be sure that the work in question is of great value and ought to be read as soon as possible. *The Possessed* (originally entitled, *The Devils*), to which the above slander was applied, is such a book. Even Maxim Gorky, a socialist who became a favorite of the regime until Stalin killed him, called Dostoyevsky's novel "slanderous and sadistic" and opposed its adaptation for the stage. On the other hand, just about anything that bears the approval and imprimatur of the Soviet Union (indeed, as everything published there must) is sure to have about as much artistic value as a kidnap note, or more appropriately, a forced recantation from the Spanish Inquisition.

The Possessed is an overstuffed book. Too many characters jostle in its pages; windy liberals, escaped convicts, drunkards, child molesters, practical jokers, comfy aristocrats and a host of others. The shifts of scene and mood are cinematically abrupt; there is an abundance of tedious small talk, especially at the beginning. It is easy to consider the work too long, although this is probably more related to the twentieth-century attention span than any literary problem.

None of this means that this is a bad book, simply that Dostoyevsky has done better.

But however crowded the cast and erratic the action, there is an iron-hard theme linking it all. *The Possessed* was, in Dostoyevsky's words, a tendentious book, and therefore a highly topical one. With good reason he chose as his epigraph the story of the Gadarene swine; his theme is the demonic nature of the revolutionary nihilism then sweeping the youth of his country. The book presents a bulging file cabinet of character studies on fanaticism. As a former member of a revolutionary socialist group, the author knew of what he wrote. But even in Russian society at large, Dostoyevsky had plenty of models to work from.

The aforementioned Sergey Nechayev, Lenin's spiritual godfather and a fanatic's fanatic if one ever existed, led a group called the People's Avengers. Nechayev murdered a fellow radical named Ivanov for reasons not entirely clear. (In any case, there need not have been a clear motive.) Dostoyevsky mentioned in a letter that he intended to use this crime in his book. He did not then proceed to write a *roman à clef*, but simply incorporated and expanded what he knew had happened. Indeed, six of Dostoyevsky's "possessed" are murdered, three die natural deaths and two commit suicide. For revolutionary fanatics such as he is describing, this is not unusual behavior. The kingpin of the bunch, Peter Verkhovensky, may be taken as Nechayev. And like Nechayev, this man knows exactly what he is doing:

> We shall proclaim destruction because—because once again the idea is so attractive for some reason! . . . I'll find you volunteers who'll be prepared to assassinate anyone and will thank you for sending them to do it. So we'll start unrest and they'll be havoc everywhere—havoc such as the world has never before witnessed.[1]

This great destruction would be preceeded by an outbreak of dehumanizing vice. This was what Verkhovensky thought was needed, along with "nice, fresh blood handy, to get them accustomed to it."[2]

What outraged the trendy set of Dostoyevsky's day was the way the author linked the fanatical band of homicidal youths with liberals. Verkhovensky sees them as serving the same purpose. The teacher who makes the children laugh at God and their families, prosecutors fearful of not being liberal enough, juries who acquit criminals and see them as "victims"—all these are "with us," says Verkhovensky, in the quest for violent upheaval and strife. Dostoyevsky saw the liberals of his day as people who tended to admire men of action. His narrator says, "A Russian liberal is bound to be a flunky who goes around looking for someone whose boots he can polish."[3] Little wonder that the left despised the book; the polemics continued long after Dostoyevsky had died.

Verkhovensky knew how to use "ready-made ideas,"— the perceived truth of the day. This consisted of propositions like: criminals are victims; religion is unimportant; a new order can be established on good intentions; to be poor is to be noble; and other such notions. He also knew how to manipulate people, a talent prevalent in John Matthys, Josef Stalin, and Charles Manson.

Shigalov, another member of the inner circle, demonstrates this as well, but is more doctrinaire. Explaining his new, all-embracing world system, he confesses that he started with unlimited freedom and wound up with unlimited despotism.[4] His social blueprint had mankind dividing mankind into two groups, an elite composed of people such as himself being one-tenth, with the other nine-tenths in abject slavery.[5] Hearing this scheme for the first time, a fellow named Lyamshin shouts that he would "grab those nine-tenths and blow them skyward!" leaving the elite to live happily ever after. The way things were actually worked out by the Bolsheviks amounted to a combination of the two plans.

What kind of person was Lyamshin? We learn that he surreptitiously slipped pornographic materials into the satchel of a woman who traveled about selling Bibles, with the result that she was humiliated (and later arrested) when they toppled out during a sale. This was his idea of a joke.

Of course it goes without saying that all the Possessed do not think highly of God. Shatov, something of a nationalist, thought that if there were an uprising it would have to begin with atheism. The trouble with atheism, comedian Mort Sahl says, is that you don't get any days off. One must always be hard at work destroying the faith of others, since most people one meets have some sort of religious belief. So Shatov was right; atheism is a good starting point.

Perhaps the most fascinating character in the book, other than the handsome, unpredictable Stavrogin, is Kirilov, a suicidal engineer who touts a Christian Atheism. (Why not? We have Christian Marxists.) He reads the book of Revelation to another member of the inner circle. Verkhovensky warns him that he may wind up inadvertently converting the man to Christianity, but this was apparently not a problem. "He's a Christian anyway," Kirilov says, "And you needn't worry, he'll slit that throat for you."[6] It thus appears that Kirilov and his friend had a little of John Bockelson in them.

But Kirilov sometimes demonstrates flashes of insight. Discussing the sort of person who could end the world, he says it would have to be a "man-god."[7] Stavrogin asks him if he doesn't mean "God-man" but Kirilov replies "man-god," providing perhaps the best definition of a fanatic ever. What Churchill said about a self-righteous colleague applies to all such types: "There, but for the grace of God, goes God."

Critics have pointed out that all Dostoyevsky's characters were not particularly accurate for the time, and perhaps this is true. But that they represent a frighteningly accurate prophecy cannot be doubted. This is what makes *The Possessed* worth reading today. The tragic dimension of these youths in a way resembles Turgenev's Bazarov. Most of them meet terrible ends, and the havoc they create is strictly regional.

But as things actually progressed, this sort of person was able to take over a full sixth of the earth and enforce a strict version of Shigalovism: the New Class ruling over the vast majority, who now must endure a new serfdom. Paul Vitz noted:

> The heroes are dead; even the anti-heroes have gone stale. The Great Revolutionary has dwindled to a part of political theater; the Communist hero is now seen as a functionary in the grim reality of the Gulag Archipelago; the socialist's ideal is a creeping bore.[8]

And as in the previous century, there currently exist many "ready-made ideas," what Orwell called "smelly little orthodoxies," just waiting to be exploited. Among these are: Socialist dictators are men of peace; capitalism is "based on greed";[9] the New York Times is a great newspaper; television anchormen are knowledgeable; abortion is a "right"; the U.N. is a valuable organization; and so on ad infinitum. This is an established order going inexorably backwards, all the while imagining that it represents "progress." Accordingly, with the fields so white to harvest, fanatics are having a field day and the man-gods rule everywhere. Hitler and Pol Pot kill their millions, Stalin his ten millions. As Dostoyevsky uncannily predicted through Verkhovensky, the earth weeps for its old gods.[10] But the new man-gods, as Kirilov imagined, may well be the pallbearers of this shabby century.

CHAPTER 11, NOTES
1. Fyodor Dostoyevsky, *The Possessed*, trans. Andrew R. MacAndrew, (New York: New American Library, 1962), 402.
2. Ibid., 400.
3. Ibid., 132-33.
4. Ibid., 384.
5. Ibid., 385.
6. Ibid., 359.
7. Ibid., 225.
8. Paul C. Vitz, *Psychology as Religion* (Grand Rapids: Eerdmans, 1977), 130.
9. This Received Idea deserves comment since the first and sometimes only statement one can elicit from Christian socialists on capitalism is that it is "based on greed." Max Weber comments that this is a "kindergarten" notion, and that greed has "nothing to do with capitalism." See Max Weber, *The Protestant Ethic and the Spirit of Capitalism*, trans. Talcott Parsons, (New York: Scribners, 1958), 17.
10. Dostoyevsky, 403.

CHAPTER 12
RASKOLNIKOV AND FRIENDS

Raskolnikov, of Dostoyevsky's *Crime and Punishment*, lives in an attic so small that he cannot open the door without getting out of bed. The story takes place in summer and the steamy, cramped quarters seem a metaphor for Raskolnikov's overheated mind.

He is a half-baked student, a proletarian Bazarov, who has recently dropped out of law school, partly for financial reasons. Dostoyevsky describes him as "superstitious" and possessed of "accumulated bitterness and contempt." Ashamed of his raggedy clothes, he keeps to himself, except for the occasional foray into a tavern—something he can ill afford.

Raskolnikov's poor fortune has made him a "monomaniac." He must skillfully avoid the landlady, and is forced to pawn the tawdriest of trinkets just to get money to eat. His dealings with Alyona Ivanovna, the pawnbroker, are humiliating. She is a miserly old woman who once savagely bit the finger of Lizaveta, her half-sister, out of pure spite. Raskolnikov hates her.

One afternoon, he hears a student and an officer discussing the old lady. Dostoyevsky records that the student "seemed to be speaking expressly for Raskolnikov." It was "as though there had really been in it something preordained, some guiding hint." What was the student saying?

"I could kill that damned old woman and make off with her money, I assure you, without the faintest conscience-prick." He adds:

> On one side we have a stupid, senseless, worthless, spiteful, ailing, horrid old woman, not simply useless but doing actual mischief, who has not an idea what she is living for herself, and who will die in a day or two in any case. . . .
>
> On the other side, fresh young lives thrown away for want of help and by thousands, on every side! A hundred thousand good deeds could be done and helped, on that old woman's money. . . .
>
> Kill her, take her money and with the help of it devote one-self to the service of humanity and the good of all. What do you think, would not one tiny crime be wiped out by thousands of good deeds? For one life thousands would be saved from corruption and decay. One death and a hundred hundred lives in exchange—it's simple arithmetic!

The same thoughts have echoed through the minds of hundreds of modern fanatics. And thoughts have consequences. As a man thinks, so is he. Without much further reflection, Raskolnikov steals an axe and murders the two women. Thereafter, *Crime and Punishment* becomes, for the most part, a detective story. But the opening chapters expose the working of the mind that hesitates not to kill for a cause.

PART
4

RANDOM SAMPLES:
General Examples of
Fanaticism in Our Time

The True Fanatic is the one who wants to save himself, and the rest of the world with him, whether or not they want to be saved. If they don't, he has no reservation about killing them, and has in fact done so, to a point that descriptions of his actions seem unbelievable. In a sense, he presents an easy target, since most of us will never be in positions of power such that the lives of many people depend on our decisions or our whims.

But fanaticism is also what happens when human beings, who are incurably religious, attempt to provide their own salvation. It may be seen as the activism of ideology, or the spirituality of secularism, or simply as excess and zealotry. The following section contains examples of this in the contemporary world.

To avoid possible misunderstanding, this author does not contend that those who are described in this part of the book are of the same character as, or sympathize with, those in the opening section. We have observed that to his quest for salvation, the True Fanatic adds absolute wickedness. Though no human being is perfect, a relatively small number may be said to exemplify such wickedness. The potential for it, I believe, lies in everyone.

The following section concerns matters closer to home, some of which touch all of us in one way or another. They deserve treatment on their own merits or demerits, and are surely open to interpretations other than those of this writer. This is particularly true of fanaticism in the arts, and is such areas as dieting.

Fanatical excesses in these areas do not mean that the practitioners deify themselves, or believe themselves infallible, or are motivated by a super-personal force, or are attempting to compensate for some perceived weakness.

However, there are cases of general fanaticism in which human beings, in quest of their own salvation, do show themselves willing or even zealous to break the homicide taboo, and hence fit the profile we have outlined. I believe it was John Donne who said that the death of every man affected him. As our first example shows, this is no small matter.

CHAPTER 13
THE SHE-ITE HOLOCAUST

Death, once invited in, leaves his muddy bootprints
everywhere.   John Updike

In A.D. 1973, seven aging men imposed abortion on
an entire country. Before that time, abortion had for the
most part been considered wrong, and unborn children were
conceded the right to life, something they no longer possess.
In the United States, the life of an unborn child may be
taken for any or no reason at any time before birth; even, in
some cases, after birth. This taking of life may be done with
complete impunity. Some parents abort their offspring because they want a child of a different sex. Others prefer that
their babies live briefly outside the womb before they are
killed so that they can claim the child for that year as a dependent for tax purposes. [1]

Since the decision of the American supreme court,
abortion has become a growth industry and popular form of
murder, whether shrouded in any of the various medical
euphemisms ("pregnancy termination service," "therapeutic," etc.) or expressed openly by people like Joseph Fletcher
as retroactive contraception or pre-natal infanticide. Whatever one's view of abortion, it cannot be denied that had the
millions of unborn children aborted since Roe v. Wade been
allowed to live, there would be some fifteen million additional people walking around in this nation today. One

wonders how many of these would have been civil-rights advocates, composers of symphonies, philanthropists, scientists dedicated to finding cures for diseases like leukemia, writers like Dorothy Sayers or Alexander Solzhenitsyn; or, even crusaders for women's rights.

Or how about religious leaders who will never see the light of day? It is highly unlikely that, under today's conditions, the birth of Jesus Christ would happen at all—in strictly human terms, of course. Mary was a young, inexperienced girl, an easy target for pro-abortion rap sessions. She was a member of a poor family to whom a child would be an economic burden, and would thus surely be urged to consider whether her offspring was really "wanted" or not. She would be led to believe that a desire to have children was a legacy of traditional, male-dominated society, a sexist belch from the past. Mary was also a member of a despised race, who, flying in the face of modernity, tended to have large families and increase the Population Explosion, that pseudo-scientific bogey of Malthusians and pop exponents of "future shock."

Worse still, the precise identity of the child's father was mysterious. Mary's claim to be pregnant by the supernatural means of the Holy Spirit could well land her in a straight jacket, or at least committed to undergo electric shock treatment. Likewise, her reports of having seen visions of angels and hearing celestial prophecies would cause concerned friends to recommend a good psychoanalyst who would doubtless perceive her "strong religious beliefs" as a problem, possibly indicative of neurosis or an "authoritarian" personality.

Should this twentieth-century Mary present herself at the local Planned Parenthood facility, all of the above conditions would certainly elicit intensive counseling with a view to achieving consent to an abortion, the payment of a substantial cash fee, then the violent death by dismemberment of her unborn child still in the womb, followed by efforts to convince her that she "had done the right thing." A modern King Herod, who ordered the deaths of male children in the hopes of eliminating Jesus, would be saved a lot of messy work.

But, thankfully, God, and the people who follow Him, are under no obligation to follow contemporary mores and trends. Mary's decision to not only go through with the pregnancy, but to consider herself blessed for doing so—and on top of that to reflect great joy because of it—would be greeted by howls of derision from the feminist pews. But Mary, I think, would prevail.

Plato wrote that in a society where licentiousness is rife, the courts are burdened and the medical clinics do a booming business. Worse still, the philosopher wrote, under these conditions the legal and medical professions begin to give themselves airs.[2] In the case of the Supreme Court decision on abortion, the appointed-for-life legal guardians of the nation simply caved in to the furious lobbying of the medical profession. A precedent: Plato would surely view this as a *trahison des clercs*, a kind of double-Judas act. The medical profession said abortion was their business; a few not very lucid old jurists, some with a tendency to doze off during the day (as Bob Woodward has described in *The Brethren*) believed them, and that was that.

The use of a wooden gallows in hanging does not make capital punishment a problem of carpentry. Neither does execution by firing squad or gas chamber make the death penalty a matter of ballistics or chemistry. Similarly, the efforts of a medical doctor "scraping it out" (a common way of describing abortion among practitioners) does not make abortion the province of the medical profession. It is a moral and spiritual issue.

In fact, the only way abortion can be considered "therapeutic" is if pregnancy is considered a disease. Doubtless, with many feminists this is the case, since, in their orthodoxy, it is not a human being in their womb, but "fetal tissue." Thus, it is their "own body" that is acting up.[3] An abortion is the only operation considered a failure if the patient lives and a success if the patient dies.

As James T. Burtchaell has pointed out in his masterful *Rachel Weeping: The Case Against Abortion*, abortion is not in any sense therapeutic for the mother either, but is frequently traumatic. His documentation of this comes primarily from books by pro-abortion feminists.

When one strays out of medicine into ethics, one discovers the contention that the unborn are "better off" if denied their first foothold in the world. Since no human being is another human being, no one has the right to make this decision for another. The law used to protect the innocent from these kinds of arbitrary decisions. It does so no longer.

It is often contended as well that the unborn are not our fellow humans. We are told, for instance, that they cannot sustain their own lives; but there are graduate students who can barely do this. A two-year-old certainly can't do it. If there is a point in the continuum of human existence when a person becomes something she was not, puberty, not birth, is a much clearer demarcation line.

Civil libertarian Aryeh Neier insists that the idea that the unborn are: a) human, b) alive, is an "act of faith"[4] This is a clear refusal to look at the evidence.

From the moment of conception, the unborn is a unique individual with her or his own genetic makeup; the heart is beating in a matter of days; the color of eyes and hair are determined. Furthermore, the unborn child can feel pain, and may be the subject of surgery while in the womb. What could be more unscientific than saying that this being is *not* human? Only an act of unreasonable faith—that is, a superstition—can hold that the unborn child is *not* human and alive. A being with a heartbeat is alive; the offspring of human beings is human, whatever stage of development he or she happens to be in.

Abortion, in addition to being a moral issue, is a religious one. (This does not mean that it is sectarian, that is, a

"Catholic issue," as abortion advocates often contend.) The term "holocaust," so accurately applied to the millions of deaths in National Socialist concentration camps, as well as, now, in abortion clinics, is a religious term. It has to do with a sacrifice consumed by fire. In the Spanish Bible the word translated in English as "sacrifice" is *holocausto*.

Viewing, then, this sanitized, legally endorsed holocaust, I cannot help but view it in purely religious terms as a wave of fanaticism seldom, if ever, paralleled in history. Beyond all the social, medical, legal and psychological cant lies this naked fact: parents are sacrificing their children to gods of their own creation. The primary definition of a fanatic—one who breaks the homicide taboo—applies here as in few other cases. Only a fanatic can kill her own children.

Feminism is really a religious gnosticism with a code of good and evil more strict than any traditional theology. Abortion is the feminists' primary station of the cross. To gain admission to the inner sanctum of she-ite hierophants, a woman must be willing to perform the sacrament. It is a rite of passage. Some women admit as much.[5]

Gloria Steinem proclaims feminism to be an integral part of socialism.[6] The millenarian vision, then, for which women are urged to kill their offspring is the standard pie-on-the earth product popular for the last half century: a society where everyone is more or less the same, anatomy notwithstanding.

Those who do sacrifice the fruit of their bodies for this vision, or for the gods of their own personal convenience—career, pleasure, the desire to express themselves, empower themselves,[7] be themselves, be "equal" or whatever—tend to fit the fanatical profile. They are by their own admission (in studies written by feminists) hostile, alienated, frightened, desperate, and often incoherent.[8]

And whatever gods they strive to please, their demonology is much stronger than their faith—the classic fanatical stance. For the radical feminist, reality is a nonstop, wide-screen newsreel of demonology, all done in Dolby

stereo. Feminist dissatisfaction with the present, with the
state of things, is nearly total. One notes their wild flights of
paranoia regarding the allegedly "well-financed" pro-life
movement. The assault forces, directed from a secret center
in the Vatican, as the feminist myth has it, are everywhere
on the march, a NATO of Catholics, the Ku Klux Klan,
Phyllis Schlaffly, fundamentalists, evangelicals, squeamish
anti-abortion doctors like C. Everett Koop, Bernard
Nathanson, and other unenlightened people. And there is
more.

The World According to Feminism is inhabited by
cruel chauvinist ogres called men. These men are engaged in
a huge, serpentine conspiracy to "tell women what they can
do with their bodies" and to "keep women down." The society they have built was "designed" for this very purpose, one
hears. But men are not the only problem.

Women are too—that is, the heathen unconverted
who stubbornly resist the light. On every hand are gender-
traitors, those distinguished non-feminists like Margaret
Thatcher or Jeanne Kirkpatrick, who have dared to achieve
distinction "within the system," and who have no use for the
class hatred of Socialism or the gender hatred of feminism.
Such ones earn the epithet "female impersonators."[9]

For women to find happiness and fulfillment in a traditional marriage and dedicate themselves to their home and
children, well, this is utter blasphemy. These ones are made
to feel miserable at every available opportunity; made to feel
as if their life is a tedious waste of time, a form of slavery, a
positive impediment to Progress. It goes without saying that
women who are active in the pro-life movement are, in this
view, the ultimate apostates.

Accordingly, the whole of human existence to a
feminist fundamentalist is "sexist," a pejorative cliche readily applied to anyone less than adoring of the feminist movement, its premises, its vocabulary, and its leaders. Civil
dialogue with these people is impossible. They talk of equality, but consider themselves superior. A good case can be

made that the only "sexists" are feminists. Imagine a "Maleist" movement, lobbying and demonstrating for "Men's Rights" and courses in "Men's Studies." Such a thing would be rightly condemned.

The feminist utopia, like all utopias, never comes. But radical feminists will continue to chase it. One suspects that no reforms would satisfy them; hence, they are locked into fantasy, frustration, and hatred. Abortion, in addition to being a sacrifice to their gods, constitutes their violent response to reality. If this is not fanaticism, then nothing is. Terrorist Carlos Marighella at least recognized that he had lost his humanity. The She-ites are the real female impersonators.

But one must not forget the physicians. In this infant Inquisition, the unborn are judged guilty of violating the doctrines of feminist religion. Their crime is that they exist. Death is their sentence. But the actual execution can present problems. In fact, it is much easier to kill a one-year-old child in the crib—or an adult in bed, for that matter—than a seven-month-old child in the womb. Here, the skill of a trained doctor is necessary.

Since Hippocrates, reverence for life has been the norm. But the medical profession has largely abandoned this position. With many doctors now routinely practicing infanticide, the doctor has reverted to his role of pagan antiquity as a killer to be feared and obeyed rather than as a healer to be trusted and respected.[10] The doctor presently serves feminist religion in two ways: as chaplain, justifying its measures; and as high priest-executioner, carrying them out in the sanitized sanctums of his clinic. For this, he is very well paid indeed.

Torquemada grew financially fat on his victims and lived in regal style. Likewise, many of the production-line slayers of National Socialism exacted fringe benefits that enabled them to retire quite comfortably in Paraguay and Argentina. The abortion holocaust, whose victims already outnumber the Inquisition and National Socialist holocaust combined, boasts entire squads of trendy Torquemadas, energetic Eichmanns, and Mercedes-driving Mengeles with fat bank accounts and stock portfolios, perhaps a condo or two in the Virgin Islands or Hawaii where they go to work off stress. As Bernard Nathanson eloquently testifies, mass killing of the unborn can exact an emotional toll, even on an upwardly-mobile secular elite.[11] What this really constitutes is metaphysical *angst*, a religious doubt. Many succeed in quashing it, and are jaded to the point of reprobation.

Nearly seventeen thousand aborted fetuses were discovered in a repossessed shipping container in Woodland Hills, California, in 1982. The trucker who opened the container was shocked to the point that he could barely speak. He actually required time off work to recover. Told that some people considered these aborted babies less than human, the man replied, "They look like people to me." To hardened abortionists and pro-abortion lobbyists like the ACLU, this is all just so much "fetal tissue" to be incinerated, not buried. They doubtless would consider the trucker's reaction as "sentimental."

Along with money, racism may be an abortion motive for some doctors. Dr. Edward Allred, whose Family Planning Associates Medical Group is responsible for over 750,000 abortions, stated in 1980 that he would do free abortions in Mexico to stem "the influx of Hispanic immigrants. Their lack of respect for democracy and social order is frightening." He added, "When a sullen black woman of 17 or 18 can decide to have a baby and get welfare and food stamps and become a burden to all of us, it's time to stop. In parts of Los Angeles, having babies for welfare is the only industry the people have."[12] Such a statement coming from Mr. Reagan would draw charges of racism. It should in this case too. In fact, Allred is being sued by the parents of a Hispanic girl, who charge that racism led to the girl's death.[13]

The unborn are the clearest case in history of innocent, helpless victims, but liberals—many Christians among them—have barred them from their honor rolls of the downtrodden and oppressed. Like Jean Calas, they deserve to be proclaimed "victims of fanaticism." Parents continue to sacrifice their unborn sons and daughters to shadowy gods, personal and collective. Doctors more often sacrifice them to Mammon.

Some in the pro-life movement are optimistic; they think the abortionists have had their day, that their time has come and gone. I hope this is true. Whether there will be a Nuremberg for abortionists in this world remains to be seen. But there will be one in the next. Of that there can be no doubt. There is nothing hidden that will not be made manifest. Fanaticism is not forever.

CHAPTER 13, NOTES

1. Tom Diaz, "IRS Asked to Explain Tax Break in Case of Abortions," *The Washington Times*, 11 January 1985.
2. *The Republic of Plato*, trans. Francis MacDonald Cornford, (New York: Oxford, 1945), 94
3. If the child is a boy, how can a woman's body have a male part?
4. James Burtchaell, *Rachel Weeping: The Case Against Abortion* (New York: Harper and Row, 1982), 111.
5. Franky Schaeffer, *A Time for Anger* (Westchester: Crossway Books, 1982), 83.
6. Tom Bethell, "What a Fool Believes," *The American Spectator*, April 1985, 9, 10.
7. Maggi Cage, who has had repeated abortions, explains, "The abortion was the first time I'd empowered myself, and I liked it so much I've been doing it ever since." Quoted in *The American Spectator*, May 1985, 46.
8. Burtchaell, 1-60.
9. Sonia Johnson quoted in Steven Hayward, "Comparable Worth?" *Chronicles of Culture*, July 1985, 11.
10. Charles Cros, in story set in the distant past, puts himself in the position of someone who wants to die, but finds this difficult because there are no doctors. See *Autrefois in Tristan Corbière: Oeuvres Completes* (Paris: Editions Gallimard).
11. Burtchaell, 197.
12. From the *San Diego Union*, 12 October 1980, quoted in *National Right to Life News*, 2 May 1985, 4.
13. Ibid.

CHAPTER 14
ACTING BEASTLY

Some members of other species are persons; some members
of our species are not. —Peter Singer

If I saw someone hurting an animal, I'd kill them.
—A California animal-rights advocate

Throughout history, people have been willing to break the homicide taboo for a number of reasons, but not for any reason. In most cases there is usually some grandiose plan for the regeneration of the world which brings on the need to eliminate those who are "in the way." In this century, some maintain these apocalyptic visions, while others seem too ready to kill for the most paltry of causes. Perhaps the latter still follow Jimmy Carter's prophecy of diminishing expectations. It seems clear that in fanaticism, as in other fields like education, there has been a general lowering of standards and entrance requirements.

In January of 1985, Dr. A.R. Moossa, of the University of California at San Diego, received an anonymous telephone call from someone who threatened to "put a bullet through his head."[1] What did the good doctor do to deserve this? Was he a heroin dealer or child molester? Not quite. Moossa's crime? He was directing a surgical training seminar that made use of anesthetized dogs. For this, someone thought he deserved death and proceeded to threaten and terrorize him in the best vigilante style.

Dr. Harvey Shapiro, another professor at the same school, received a letter informing him that he was on a "hit list." Then, on October 26, 1984, another letter arrived containing a picture of the doctor with rifle-scope cross hairs centered on his face. An accompanying poem read: "Roses are red, violets are blue; lab animals don't stand a chance—and from now on, neither do you."[2] Shortly after this, a group identifying itself as the Animal Liberation Front (ALF) vandalized Shapiro's house and left a jack-o'-lantern full of dog dung on his doorstep. (A nice, stylistic flourish.) Neither doctor has been harmed, but both they and the FBI take the threats very seriously. Because these incidents occurred in California, a place notable for extremists, it may appear that this is a regional issue. But this is not at all the case.

The ALF and other animal-rights groups (henceforth to be called "animalists" for the sake of brevity and accuracy) like the Guardian Apes are not regional but international. Many researchers in North America and abroad have been threatened with death, and entire projects aiming at cures for cancer, herpes, and AIDS have been sabotaged and ruined. While, as of this writing, no one has been murdered, one can with some confidence predict that this will eventually take place. Fanatics usually manage to deliver the goods they promise. Failing to take them seriously is a great mistake. But one thing is certain: human beings have already suffered because of this destruction and violence. This is a crusade whose time has come, and which will soon affect everyone, not just medical scientists.

One regards the self-image of animalists with breathless admiration. Peter Singer, an ethicist and patriarch of the movement, regards the cause as egalitarian. Ingrid Newkirk of People for the Ethical Treatment of Animals (PETA), sees animal rights as "revolutionary," a continuation of the struggle that freed slaves and won full civil rights for black Americans. Tom Regan, author of *The Case for Animal Rights*, equates his cause with everything noble in history.

Animal-rights activists readily assemble themselves for a group picture with Spartacus, Wilberforce, Abraham Lincoln and Martin Luther King, Jr. None of these venerable gentleman is alive to explain what they think of the comparison between, say, gaining liberty for an enslaved people and vandalizing hospitals where medical research takes place. But it is possible to guess what their reaction might be.

This exalted self-image very definitely fits the fanatical profile in which one sees oneself as swept along by a superpersonal force—in this case, the tide of "progressive" history. The animal-rights activist harbors no doubts that she (there are more women than men in the movement) is one of the Vanguard, a member of the Elect, helping to bring true righteousness to the world.

Unfortunately, the objectives of the animal-rights crusade are often overlooked, even by those critical of the movement. The "ethical" treatment of animals really means a complete halt to all use of animals in medical research, and an end to all use of animals for food. When one thinks about this for more than a few moments it becomes apparent that what we are dealing with is a tiny, vociferous minority attempting, in South African style, to impose its extremist beliefs on the majority. But then, fanatics are seldom fond of democracy, except for its practice of letting them speak their mind.

Obviously, banning the use of animals for research and food is a completely unrealistic goal, especially in a democratic political system; unless, of course, the majority decides to halt fifty years of medical progress or become overnight converts to Seventh Day Adventism or vegetarianism. One might just as well sit down with Karl Marx and wait for the state to wither away. It is not going to happen. I asked a member of PETA if any existing societies modeled the principles and ideals of the animalist movement. She said that none did, confirming that the movement is utopian. Utopia literally means "no place."

The vision of animalists is a kind of social gnosticism,

an unrealistic, unattainable program, striven for nonetheless with great militancy. When people labor on behalf of a utopia, fanaticism generally results.

PETA numbers some 30,000 people in the United States. Though they advocate peaceful methods for their cause—lobbying, letter-writing, picketing etc.—they are also the public relations organization for the Animal Liberation Front. PETA is related to the ALF the way Sinn Fein, a political organization, is related to the IRA (Irish Republican Army).

Ingrid Newkirk of PETA freely admits that the vast majority of her organization are vegetarian, and that their goal is to stop all use of animals for food. Given this, is it unreasonable to expect threats and attacks on farmers who raise animals for food? Tom Regan believes that animals have enforceable claims against humans, and that farmers who raise animals for food should be jailed.[3]

Since legislation of this sort is simply not going to happen (and even if it did, it would be impossible to enforce), why should not the underground "liberators" of the ALF use this as a pretext to dish out their own brand of violent justice against the cruel, unjust, "establishment"? After all, they have the widest variety of bull's-eyes: grocery stores, fast-food outlets, perhaps even a grade-school student caught red-handed with a Big Mac or Whopper. The fanatic always prefers demolition to construction. It matters not who suffers, as long as the cause is served.

Animalists, for all their talk of rights and compassion, display a blatant insensitivity to human suffering. After the ALF stole dogs from a University of California research center in 1983 (note: dogs suffered because of this), many sympathizers called and suggested that people—"welfare bums"—be experimented on, not animals.[4] Likewise, an AIDS project at the University of California at Davis has been attacked for favoring the victims of AIDS, who, they say, deserve their fate, which, by this reasoning, makes the use of research chimps unjust.

It should be noted that AIDS does not effect only homosexuals, but some heterosexuals as well. Do these people deserve their fate?

Walter C. Randall of the Loyola Medical School says, "We can trace virtually every modern medical miracle back to original studies in animals."[5] These include immunizations for polio, diphtheria, and diabetes. Surgical procedures resulting from animal research include coronary bypass, joint replacement, and kidney and liver transplants. Not only have these surgeries and serums saved the lives of thousands of people the world over, but have benefited both wild and farm animals as well. But the animal-rights advocates, from Peter Singer on down, would rather have people suffer than animals. The people who believe this have a personal problem. This is cruelty; this is fanaticism.

It is interesting that some very prominent fanatics already examined in this book showed the same ambivalence about the relative value of human and animal life. And while we must avoid any logic promoting guilt-by-association—"you are a vegetarian, therefore you are a fanatic"—this historical detail is interesting. Charles Manson, who had no qualms about murdering humans, was himself a vegetarian and a strong believer in animal rights.[6] He also would "rather kill people than animals."[7]

Lenin, a man who spoke with great delight of sweeping, merciless destruction of human beings, of massive "liquidations," could not bring himself to shoot a fox "because it was so beautiful."[8]

Hitler, who regarded Jews as a kind of social infection, was a teetotaler, nonsmoker and a vegetarian.[9] Albert Speer, a member of the National Socialist inner circle, reported that Hitler's Alsatian dog, Blondi, "remained the only living creature at headquarters who aroused any flicker of human feeling in Hitler."[10] In comparing Hitler's relations with humans and animals, Speer observed that Blondi "occupied the most important role in Hitler's private life."[11] Malcolm Muggeridge once noted rather cynically that if

Hitler's National Socialist Reich had treated kittens, spaniels, and beagles the way they treated Jews, England would have entered the war earlier.

Spanish philosopher José Ortega y Gasset writes in his book *Meditations on Hunting* that during the Spanish Civil War, a notoriously bloody conflict, an English woman offered money for ambulances to care for the many wounded. When it came to carrying out the plan, it turned out that the woman had intended the ambulances not for wounded soldiers, but for dogs. [12]

I asked Lucy Shelton of PETA what she would do if she witnessed an accident in which a five-year-old girl and a beagle had both been hurt. Which one would she help first? She had to think about this for quite a long time, and finally said "I'd have to see which one needed it more." I also asked her if there were not more important causes than animal rights, daring to mention abortion. "I've never thought about that," she said. In our strange world, it is the opponents of capital punishment and the killing of seals who are indifferent to the killing of unborn babies. Indifferent, perhaps, as well to the murder of scientists.

The animalist cause also fits the definition of fanaticism as activated superstition. The superstition behind animalism is a kind of all-pervasive equality which argues that there should be no difference in the rights accorded to people and animals. [13] Peter Singer explains, in a passage that should be read aloud several times, as slowly as possible:

> Hence we should reject the doctrine that places the lives of members of our own species above the lives of members of other species. Some members of other species are persons: some members of our own species are not. No objective assessment can give greater value to the lives of members of our species who are not persons than to the lives of members of other species who are. On the contrary, as we have seen, there are strong arguments for placing the lives of persons above the lives of nonpersons. So it seems that killing, say, a chimpanzee is worse than the killing of a gravely defective human who is not a person. [14]

Elsewhere, Singer identifies these human beings "who are not persons" as those who are severely handicapped or retarded.[15] Animal-rights advocates contend that they are not in an either-or position, that by improving the lot of animals, everybody benefits. But in the case of Singer, who is positively revered by PETA and other groups, it is obvious that his elevated view of animals has already lowered his view of human beings. His use of the Orwellian "nonperson" for someone who can't "think and talk as normal humans do,"[16] belies this. If regarding a human being, however "defective," as a nonperson does not lower his or her value, it is hard to imagine what might.

Just as Marxists and feminists glibly disparage the whole of human civilization as "bourgeois" and "sexist" respectively, animalists call those who disagree with them "speciesists," used in the sense of "racist." The parents of a handicapped child who believe their offspring has more value than a monkey are thus bigoted "speciesists," as are those of us (viz., the vast majority of the human race throughout history) who use animals for food.

Human beings are only equal before God and the law. In other respects, equality simply does not exist; it is a superstition. I cannot play basketball as well as Michael Jordan; Gloria Steinem is more articulate than Jesse Helms; Mark Hatfield is more compassionate that Augusto Pinochet; John Kenneth Galbraith is taller, and probably more erudite, than Willie Shoemaker. In speculating on what system would best serve the interests of his kind of equality, Singer trots out the Marxist slogan: "From each according to his ability, to each according to his needs."

This system presupposes and demands a dictatorship. Notice the first words: *from each*. And as a reading of *Animal Farm* coupled with a survey of Marxist countries shows, under this arrangement the pigs inevitably take over. Thus, Singer rejects and mocks Christianity and the biblical idea of the primacy of man; he has no trouble with the primacy of a Marxist dictatorship in which some people are definitely more equal than others.

In their utopian dreams, animalists see themselves heading up a posse, rounding up those using animals to find a cure for something like leukemia. They envision themselves bringing in the culprits—those who raise beef cattle—to the cheers of the vegetarian masses. They see themselves as judges in televised show trials of those who committed the atrocity of using dogs to discover insulin. There is no doubt in their minds that they are the purveyors of an age of righteousness. It is a religious reverie.

It is also, in fact, staunch neo-pantheism, a religious view in which all life—even plant life—has equal value. Margaret Bosch Van Drakestein believes that turtles are psychic.[17] Said vegetarian Nellie Shriver, coordinator of an anti-lawn mowing campaign:

> It's impossible to mow grass without harming it. We believe
> grass has some sort of consciousness, that it has feelings.[18]

How can one hold a discussion with someone who believes it is wrong to mow a lawn? Of course, if grass has feelings, then so does wheat and barley and other things people eat. Even Hinduism, which tolerates sacred cows ambling among starving humans, cannot match this kind of statement for sheer fanatical absurdity.

In an often-repeated vignette from a once-popular cartoon, a determined coyote chases a roadrunner off a cliff. The swift, winged roadrunner easily gains the far ridge. The speciesist coyote, hungry for fowl, follows for a space on sheer momentum, but eventually looks down, and, finding nothing underneath, plunges to the canyon floor. This forms a parable of sorts.

The late Francis Schaeffer pointed out that Western civilization has been running on memories of Judeo-Christian ethics, which include the primacy of man. The animalist movement is a sign that these memories are almost completely spent. Under these conditions, what can happen?

The valiant Nellie Shriver, with her picket sign denouncing those cruel thugs who mow their lawns, is at least attempting to take her premises a little farther along, though not nearly far enough. Novelist D. Keith Mano, in a most sagacious book, *The Bridge*, takes the egalitarian animal-rights premises to their final destination. He describes a world run by an animal-rights dictatorship. All taking of life is forbidden. In the year 2035, the rulers come to an important decision worth quoting in full:

> DECREE OF THE COUNCIL IN FULL,
> PASSED UNANIMOUSLY
> July 7, 2035
>
> Whereas it has been ascertained irrefutably by the Council's Committee on Respiration that the process of breathing has and will continue to destroy and maim innumerable forms of microscopic biological life, we of the Council, convened in full, have decided that man in good conscience can no longer permit this wanton destruction of our fellow creatures, whose right to exist is fully as great as ours. It is therefore decreed that men, in spontaneous free will and contrition, voluntarily accede to the termination of their species.
>
> This decree will be carried out finally not later than July 20, 2035 by all private citizens; not later than Aug. 1, 2035 by all officers of the Council.
>
> It is hoped brethren, that you will donate your physical bodies to the earth in such a manner that the heinous crimes of murder and pollution committed by our race throughout history may in some small way find redress.
>
> Go now in peace and love. [19]

The dominant force of this age is not inevitable progress, but a death wish. This is what ultimately underlies animalism: an abandonment of divinely mandated primacy for women and men, a weariness with being human.

As Hippolyte Taine pointed out, there is nothing more dangerous than a general idea in narrow, empty minds. Peter Singer and Tom Regan provide the general idea—that a warthog has the same rights as, say, Mother Teresa or Bishop

Desmond Tutu—and the ALF provides the narrow, fanatical minds. One result is that some people act very beastly indeed.

And all of us will be affected because animalism is moving from strength to strength. It is an easy movement to join; anyone can mouth its pantheistic pieties. It is an easy, no cost way to seize the moral high ground. Animalism has even moved into mainstream politics. California state senator David Roberti (D. Hollywood) sponsored a bill prohibiting the use of pound animals in research (it was defeated). Roberti operates a political action committee that will only bankroll those candidates who support animal rights.

The electronic media give animal-rights groups much free publicity and often slant their reports in favor of groups like PETA. They show emotional footage of animals undergoing tests, but never show a six-year-old girl dying of cystic fibrosis. (Perhaps, like Peter Singer, they consider such ones as "nonpersons.") In coverage of animalism, the media seldom include testimonies of people who owe their very lives to animal research. In any case, this does not "play" as well as shouting protesters. The benefits of medical research are similarly difficult to translate to the screen. But battered animals gain quick attention. The visual media will always be biased on this issue.

Animalism is a crusade that serves to increase human suffering in the name of a utopian egalitarianism, that thrives on spiritual emptiness, that brands its opponents "speciesists," and in some cases indulges in terrorism and death threats. This movement is certain to grow in strength. General ideas are the worst of all tyrants.

CHAPTER 14, NOTES
1. "60 Protest Use of Dogs for Surgery," *San Diego Union*, 20 January 1985.
2. Rex Dalton, "Animal Rights Issue Heats Up," *San Diego Union*, 25 November 1984.
3. David Kirp, "Do Animals Have Rights," *Sacramento Bee*, 16 January 1984.
4. Ibid.

5. See Lloyd Billingsley, "Save the Beasts, Not the Children?" *Eternity*, February 1985, 34.

6. Vincent Bugliosi, *Helter Skelter* (New York: Norton, 1974), 224.

7. Ibid., 289.

8. Robert Payne, *The Life and Death of Lenin* (New York: Avon Books, 1964), 88.

9. William Shirer, *The Rise and Fall of the Third Reich* (New York: Simon and Schuster, 1961), 14.

10. Albert Speer, *Inside the Third Reich* (New York: Avon Books, 1971), 392. Functionaries in the Nazi genocidal *apparat* also displayed the same callousness to human life coupled with gentleness toward animals. An official at Ravensbruck routinely tortured women but was described as a man "who could do no harm to any animal" and who, when a relative's canary died, improvised a coffin and buried the bird under a rosebush in the garden. See Rudolf Hess, *Commandant of Auschwitz*, trans. Constantine FitzGibbon (New York: World, 1959), 25.

11. Ibid., 390.

12. José Ortega y Gasset, *Meditations on Hunting*, trans. Howard Westcott (New York: Scribners, 1972), 107.

13. One wonders what animalists think of bestiality. Is it another case of animal rights being violated? Or is it the strongest possible statement of equality between the species?

14. Peter Singer, *Practical Ethics* (Cambridge: Cambridge University Press, 1979), 97.

15. Ibid., 73.

16. Ibid.

17. Margaret Bosch Van Drakestein, "Are Tortoises Psychic?" *The Ark*, 42 (August 1984): 48-49.

18. Nellie Shriver, quoted in "Voices Better Left Unsaid," *Life*, January 1985, 72.

19. D. Keith Mano, *The Bridge* (New York: Doubleday, 1973), 65.

CHAPTER 15
EROTOMANIA

Sex is so very important; it is probably the most important
thing. What is more important? I know of nothing.
                                                    —Gay Talese

"Travel Air Otica ['erotica']. We fly you everyplace, but we
get you nowhere."
                                    —From the movie, *All That Jazz*

Once widely regarded as sinful, sex has attained a
sparkling status as a new, universal Way to Salvation, proclaimed by pipe-puffing, pajama-ed messiahs like Hugh
Hefner, gold-chain bedecked porn mandarins like Bob
Guccione, and erotic evangelists like Gay Talese. This Way
of Salvation has seen mass conversions in our time, especially in the USA, where the disastrous phrase, "pursuit of
happiness," is often taken as a constitutionally guaranteed
Right to Sexual Bliss for every citizen. As he has done so
often, Malcolm Muggeridge saw this all coming a long time
ago, predicting that sex would become the "obsessive quest
of our restless and confused generation."[1]

An eager acolyte himself at one time, Muggeridge imagined that the moving stairway of sex could lead one into a
paradise where ecstasy was attainable by sensation, pure and
undefiled. His own struggles with the issue were worked out
in his book, *In a Valley of This Restless Mind*, a highly stylized
autobiographical novel dealing with the subject of lust,

which the author, then and now, views as a kind of *ersatz* faith. When the book was reissued in 1978, he explained in a new introduction:

> Of the Seven Deadly Sins, Lust is the only one which makes any serious appeal to the Imagination, as distinct from the Will, eroticism being a sort of *ersatz* transcendentalism which can easily be mistaken for the genuine article.[2]

A reviewer of the book correctly discerned Muggeridge's thesis that love and lust are antithetical, and that lust is boring.[3]

Erotomania, then, in this analysis, is one of the booming religions of our time. "To be carnally minded is life," proclaims its fundamental principle; or, to paraphrase, "Sex Saves." As Hoffer observed, when the individual must do his own soul saving, he is at it twenty four-hours a day. The eruption of sexual fanaticism Hoffer spoke of is well under way, carried to a pitch of absurdity never before equaled. This self-help religion sets up shrines everywhere; its icons, on celluloid or glossy paper, are nearly omnipresent. Walker Percy has commented that this is the most eroticized society in history.[4] Few, if anyone, would argue.

The progenitor of this erotic cult was probably D.H. Lawrence, with special mention to Havelock Ellis, Henry Miller, and, of course, Sigmund Freud. Lawrence's compilation of phallic fantasies, *Lady Chatterley's Lover*, so enriched its publisher that his shares were referred to on the London Stock Exchange as "Chatterleys."[5] It is dubious whether Lawrence would have approved of the flood of high-tech pornography that has followed; he likely would have found it abhorrent. But movements pass away from their founders; they divide, splinter and proliferate. Onward it goes, the prevailing transcendentalism of our time, and a profitable one at that.

Questions arise. Is not the sexual drive, as currently expressed, merely one of our basic biological needs? If so, then why are films, advertisements, and the cover of *Penthouse* magazine not decked out with roasted turkeys, hams, and sumptuous desserts instead of generously endowed and erotically posed human bodies?

A parallel may be drawn with Marxism-Leninism. If it is inevitable that the downtrodden masses will rise in violent revolt, why so much effort at consciousness-raising by propagandists? What the busy evangelists of socialism and erotomania are both after is far from the natural order of things.

Unlike other biological needs such as food, drink, and rest, the sex drive peaks early in life, then inexorably declines. Evelyn Waugh, author of *Brideshead Revisited* and certainly no Moral Majoritarian, comments:

> Sex instinct in most cases is a perfectly mild and controllable appetite which would never cause most of us any serious trouble at all if it was not being continually agitated by every sort of hint and suppression. Even in the case of peculiarly fiery natures, the sex interest only predominates for about half the active life.[6]

To many sexologists—the clergy of erotomania—this statement of the obvious amounts to blasphemy. But the fanatical mindset is never happy with the way things are.

Or how about the Darwinian view, that the current sexual mania is merely an up-to-date rendition of the struggle for perpetuation of the species and survival of the fittest? If this is so, then why is so much human sexual behavior—anal and oral sex, masturbation,[7] all homosexual activity—totally unrelated to human reproduction and the survival of the species? A Silver Springs, Maryland man needed rabies treatment after making love to a raccoon[8], which may, in fact, have been dead. What do necrophilia and bestiality, which are combined in this admittedly bizarre case, have to do with the perpetuation of the human race?

People have indulged their sex drive and advanced the human race since time immemorial. None of this required the sexual fanaticism of the current century. At present, other factors are involved.

The once common phrase, "sexual revolution," is seldom used anymore, although a revolution of sorts is still in process. Every revolution needs its myth-makers, and the prophets of the sexual revolution were clear on what they were against. "We were fighting against dark, traditional values of the church, the family, old morals and institutions,"[9] says Rita Liljestrom, a Swedish sociologist. The Enemy was The Past, The Church; its sexual mores, along with everything else it had wrought, had to be eliminated. People had to be "liberated." This whole dialectic was clearer in defining its demonology than what it actually desired; it was millenarian and utopian in outlook; in other words, it constitutes the classic stance of fanaticism in which demolition takes precedence over construction. Little wonder it should be fanatical and destructive in practice.

Sweden, above all places, has taken steps to establish a sexual utopia. It became in the sixties and seventies a libidinous lotus land stocked with statuesque blondes, government-sanitized against venereal disease, chemically protected against adverse affects like birth, and ready to "perform sex" just on general principles. Or, as is often the case, for money. With contraceptives distributed everywhere, prostitution, pornography, and abortion made legal, and tiny tots given sex classes in school when they had barely mastered the multiplication table, erotomania practically replaced Lutheranism as the state religion. Before the result of all this could be effectively gauged, other societies were falling all over themselves to do the same thing.

In the United States, *New Yorker* film critic Pauline Kael writes of a brutally sadomasochistic movie, "it was good enough to touch greatness."[10] *Taxi zum Klo* (Taxi to the Toilet), a hard-core homosexual film whose title says it all (as well as pinpointing where it belongs) was described by Richard Corliss of *Time* magazine as, "Witty, charming, rigorously unsentimental."[11] A professor of renaissance literature testified in court that the X-rated film *Caligula* contained "more historicity" than one of Shakespeare's plays, and also had "educational value."[12]

Magazines like *Esquire*, which once published writers like Evelyn Waugh and Thomas Mann, now print articles on the sexual merits of the vibrator. Prestigious book clubs have offered tomes like *The Joy of Gay Sex* (and, in the interests of gender balance, *The Joy of Lesbian Sex*) as "stocking stuffers" for Christmas.

Cable television systems, in addition to R and X-rated fare, feature Dr. Ruth Westheimer's *Good Sex*, a prime-time airing of sexual problems and advice that some television critics have assailed as just another form of porn, like phone sex.

Who is more arduous in pursuit of Salvation by Sex than homosexuals? Though not all are promiscuous, many admit to hundreds of sexual encounters every year, thousands over a lifetime, most with strangers. When the Pope, who speaks out against homosexuality, visited Holland in 1985, mobs of homosexuals and punk rockers rioted, shouting profanities and chanting, "Kill the Pope!" They even sang, "We'll kill, kill, kill, the Pope tonight," to the tune of "Rock Around the Clock."[13] Would these people have made good their threat and broken the homicide taboo if given the chance, thus qualifying as True Fanatics? I think so.

This trend is far from secular. In the classified section of *Ms.* magazine one finds ads placed by lesbian Adventists. There are also lesbian nuns[14] and lesbian evangelicals. One also comes across militant groups like Presbyterians for Gay/Lesbian Concerns.

Sex manuals written by Christian authors advocate forms of sado-masochism and transvestism, anal sex, and even the use of vibrators.[15] Popular books like Marabel Morgan's *The Total Woman*, while ostensibly "manuals," are really pornography.

Sex has even replaced "progress" or the "class struggle"

as a way of interpreting people and events. Political cartoonist Jules Feiffer, who has lectured at the Washington Institute for Policy Studies, theorizes that good politicians were people with "sexual energy." Franklin Roosevelt was "strong, vital, attractive, and in a wheel chair. Perfect! Safe sexual energy." Feiffer compared him to Jon Voight in the movie *Coming Home*. The Second World War would have been lost, he believes, "if FDR were not sexy."[16] Truman, on the other hand, "lacked sex" and thus "had to resort to Atom Bombs." But not to worry, Eisenhower radiated a "post coital glow." And LBJ?—"Raw, unharnessed sexual energy. It was as if Vietnam was a venereal by-product of LBJ's sex drive, banging away to keep his dominoes up."[17] In similar fashion, anti-nuclear warrior Helen Caldicott cites "missile envy" as a cause for the "arms race."

All these people—heterosexual, homosexual, married, single, all the way down to the troubled chap fornicating with a dead raccoon—are on the same moving stairway of sexual sacraments described by Muggeridge; ascending to no heights, descending to no depths, but ardently pursuing Salvation through pure sensual ecstasy. Advertising pitchmen know this, and exploit it to the full.

"Now," reads an ad for the book, *The G Spot*, "a fascinating new book tells how these women—and many others—discovered a source of sexual pleasure so intense, so satisfying that *it virtually changed their lives* (italics added). The implied pitch, blatantly religious, is: this can change your whole life! You can be a new you! A list of testimonies follows.

"I really feel free and think I can relax and maybe express myself more now," says an Alabama woman.

"I wouldn't trade this sensation for the world," another lady adds.

The notion of any physical sensation providing such a change in one's life is a fantasy. But fantasy is a strong sacrament of erotomania. There are no real people like the actors in pornographic films. (Or, for that matter, like actors in

practically any film.) The airbrushed beauties, forever panting and forever young, in the glossy pages of *Penthouse* are,
like the flawless faces on the covers of fashion magazines, an
illusion.

The Swedes, first in the Promised Land, are finding
that all is not well. Hans Nestius of the Swedish Association
for Sex Education, who fought for the legalization of pornography, now condemns it as destructive. Doctor C. Elthammer
of the Stockholm Child Psychiatric Department set out to
prove that pornography does not have a corrupting effect.
He arranged for some children between the ages of eleven
and eighteen to see a film of a woman being gang-raped then
forced to have sex with a dog. Some of the girls did admit to
being shocked, but two adults who were present needed psychiatric treatment for a month. [18]

Sociologist Liljestrom now denounces the sexual revolution as a "pseudo-liberation" that causes "alienation." [19]
No people in the world seek mental health counseling more
than the Swedes. What is their most common complaint?

Maj-Brihit Bergstrom-Walan directs the Swedish Institute for Sexual Research. She reports that the prevailing
angst in her country is, of all things, a lack of sex drive. [20] In
a sexually-obsessed society, sex itself loses importance.

A curiosity in all this is that the Judeo-Christian view
of sex, so derided by sexual revolutionaries is really, when all
things are considered, a middle-of-the-road stance. In the
Judeo-Christian tradition, sex has its obvious reproductive
function but is also an expression of love between marriage
partners. For this reason it is to be kept within the marriage
bond. Within this bond, whatever sexual behavior is not
physically or psychologically harmful, and mutually agreed
on by both partners, is acceptable. This is a long way from
medieval, sub-Christian views of sex as inherently sinful; a
long way, too, from the pacts of virginity within marriage
that were once known in Europe.

But the Judeo-Christian view is also far removed from
the modern Sex as Salvation mania. It sees sex not as

something mechanical that can be solved by technique or special aids, but something mysterious and sacred that belongs to the realm of true human love. The Judeo-Christian tradition, then, avoids all extremes. It postulates that sex is a good servant, but a poor master; also that sex without love is a lot closer to hell than heaven.

Those who have attacked the Judeo-Christian tradition as repressive or puritanical are, like Don Quixote, tilting at windmills. But the fanatic, however calm and educated, attacks not because something merits attacking, but because of problems of his own.

The spiritual void inside human beings cannot be filled with sensation, just as it cannot be filled with things, or money, or prestige. To repeat Augustine's question: if God Himself cannot satisfy you, what will? Will sex with oneself, or with a famous actress or actor, or with two or three at the same time, or on a Supersonic Concorde, or drug-aided? Wouldn't this fling one into a sensual paradise unspoiled by commitment, pregnancy, and children?

But this utopia, like all others, never comes. It always lies just out of reach, forever visible and beckoning. The sex god is a hollow golden calf that often mocks its most eager supporters, demanding of them increased sacrifices. How many sexual zealots are now so jaded that they can only be satisfied by saturnalias, or rape, or child pornography, or the sadistic molestation of children?

The true sexists are all those who pursue salvation through eroticism. Though much evidence shows that this relentless quest leads to satiety, disgust, and even cruelty, those engulfed in it show few signs of diminishing their fanatical zeal.

CHAPTER 15, NOTES
1. Malcolm Muggeridge, *Chronicles of Wasted Time* (New York: Morrow, 1973), 142.
2. Malcolm Muggeridge, *In a Valley of This Restless Mind* (London: Collins, 1978), 10.

3. Evelyn Waugh, "Desert Islander," a review of Muggeridge's *Valley* in *The Essays, Articles and Reviews of Evelyn Waugh*, (Boston: Little, Brown, 1984), 233.

4. Walker Percy, *Lost in the Cosmos* (New York: Washington Square Press, 1983), 14.

5. Muggeridge, *Chronicles of Wasted Time*, 66.

6. Waugh, 95.

7. Woody Allen best brings out the narcissistic nature of masturbation in his film *Annie Hall*. "Don't knock masturbation," he says. "It's most people's only chance to have sex with someone they really love."

8. R. Emmett Tyrrell, "The Continuing Crisis," *The American Spectator*, May 1985, 4.

9. Robert Sarner, "Fallout from the Sexual Revolution," *MacLean's* 12 January 1981, 7.

10. Bryan Griffin, *Panic Among the Philistines* (Chicago: Regnery Gateway, 1983), 14.

11. Ibid., 182.

12. Ibid., 139.

13. Don A. Schanche, "Hundreds Riot During Pope's Visit," *Los Angeles Times*, 13 May 1985, 1.

14. Ann Japenga, "Lesbians Coming Out of Cloisters," *Los Angeles Times*, 1 May 1985.

15. Robert M. Price, "You Must Be Porn Again," *The Wittenburg Door*, April-May 1981, 28.

16. Griffin, 154.

17. Ibid.

18. Recorded in Malcolm Muggeridge, *Christ and the Media* (Grand Rapids: Eerdmans, 1977), 27, 8.

19. Sarner, 8.

20. Ibid.

CHAPTER 16
FAN APPRECIATION

American sportscaster Bob Costas, when asked why he carried around a baseball card of Mickey Mantle, replied that one should always have a religious artifact on one's person at all times. Though spoken half in jest, there is a strong dimension of truth in this religiofication of sports.

In fact, the purest modern derivation of the term *fanaticus* is "fan," shorthand for fanatic. This is no etymological accident. In the modern scene, the temple with its oracles has been replaced by the stadium with its gladiators. In ancient, pagan times, these two were never too far separated. Other religious terminology has been adapted wholesale. Certain players are certified "legends" and eventually find themselves subjected to a vote every bit as complicated as the election of a new Pope. Sometimes, not always on the first ballot, the puffs of journalistic smoke emerge and the public is told that the player in question has been sanctified from the rank and file and become forever enshrined in the Hall of Fame as a "sports immortal."

Statistics are cited in support of various candidates for this athletic immortality. The debate involving this confetti of numbers is often as heated and dogmatic as a front-door theological argument with a cult representative. Even fans of scant intellectual distinction become suddenly capable of prodigious feats of memory when it comes to a batting average. The process resembles the quoting of a favorite Bible verse in support of a pet doctrine.

Athletes have become the primary role models for young people. Basketball stars—not playwrights, philosophers, priests, missionaries, theologians, or novelists—appear in television spots warning the young of the dangers of alcohol and drugs. Why do this if these players are not widely venerated? Even churches searching for an exemplary banquet speaker in many cases choose a famous athlete with religious convictions. A dedicated life worthy of emulation is somehow not enough by itself; one must also be a sports figure.

That sports can be helpful in developing teamwork, discipline, fitness, and sacrifice is not in question here. But it should be noted that these qualities derive more from participation than observation.

Sports is also a legitimate facet of the entertainment business. People operating under the pressures of modern society sometimes need a catharsis. Yelling oneself hoarse at a game can be healthy. But the present state of affairs nearly defies the word "excess." Western societies are glutted with sports.

Television has a great deal to do with this. Television did for sports what the automobile and drive-in theatre did for sexual immorality. This has led to masses of people becoming full-fledged voyeurs, living vicariously through the actions of others. On just about any given day, in the privacy of one's living room, one may watch football, basketball, hockey, baseball, lacrosse, track and field, full contact karate, boxing, soccer, curling, Australian rules football, rugby, badminton, tennis, bowling, car racing, jai alai, motocross, volleyball, and others, not to mention the multitudinous Olympic events, including esoteric contests like equestrianism. Strung together, the various leagues form an elongated eye-chart: NL, AL, NBA, NHL, PKA, WBC,

USFL, CFL, NCAA, FIFA, ACC, MISL and many others. Why are there so many takers, as the advertising rates verify?

This eruption of sports is surely a response to a massive spiritual void coupled with the *ennui* so characteristic of affluent societies. For various reasons, many lives lack excitement, thrills, and a "good versus evil" struggle with clearly defined villains. Televised wrestling,[1] currently riding a wave of popularity, serves as a parable for all spectator sports in its role as a vendor of myths.

Wrestling promoters provide a whole pantheon of Agents of Darkness and Knights in Shining Armor. There are Heroes and People You Love to Hate. It matters not that the good guys are showered with attention then relegated to the slag heap of obscurity. There is always a fresh supply. But it is all aimed at a genuine need. With much fluff and buffoonery in literature and film, and with the stage so paralyzingly topical, wrestling is becoming the prevailing forum for the dramatization of good versus evil.

The church—especially its theological liberals—has helped this by demythologizing the devil, which frees him to work as a deep cover agent, often in ecclesiastical ranks. Personal evil is called psychosis, or neurosis. National struggles are a simple matter of getting our welfare services right and building a day-care center and abortion clinic beside every convenience store. Western culture, as trendy clergy have it, has no antagonists or enemies, just "social problems." And with so many churches—especially the mainline Protestant variety—being dry and lifeless as the Gobi and just about as empty, the attraction of a clapping, chanting crowd, shrieking for the Heroes to vanquish the Ungodly is obvious. This is how one has "fellowship." It is better to go out to church (or to the arena) than to worship at home.

For a highly secularized populace of spiritual anorexics, the idea of victory has been removed from the transcendent realm to the transient or material world. Those who confect sports for public consumption are selling a salvation of sorts: victory vicariously achieved on the playing field or in the ring. The bored, sedentary fan who is or feels himself to be of little value, sitting in his lounge chair, six pack of Miller and bag of chips at his side, thus acquires the right to hoist his finger and shout to the world, "We're number one! We're number one!"

Just how important this pseudo-religion of vicarious triumph is may be seen in the lengths its adherents will go to defend it. Fans of opposing teams are often subjected to abuse or even deadly attacks, an athletic *jihad*. In May of 1985, before the soccer match for the European cup between Liverpool of England and Juventus of Italy, English fans attacked a group of Italians. Thirty-eight people perished. Explaining all this, sociologists may cite poverty or unemployment. Jack Lang, the French minister of culture, speaking on national television in France, blamed the soccer deaths on Margaret Thatcher.[2] Psychiatrists may cite mass hysteria or national chauvinism. Temperance lobbies see proof of the dangers of alcohol.

Writer Alfie Kohn sees "the system" as faulty; he believes competition itself is to blame.[3] This latter interpretation is far from new, a regurgitation of the notion that violent fanatics, far from being dangerous individuals, are themselves "victims" of an "unjust (read 'free enterprise') society." This view has helped fanaticism to flourish by absolving guilty individuals of responsibility for their actions.

Mass hysteria, alcohol abuse, and nationalism may well have played a role in the soccer deaths in Belgium, but when people are willing to break the homicide taboo for an abstraction, one can be sure that fanatics are hard at work. Chaos is the element in which they thrive. These outbreaks of violence are examples of "fans" living up to their name.

But the athletes themselves cannot be exempted. In both East and West, sports has become a branch of veterinary medicine. Athletes are set apart and reared like racehorses, or *castrati* for the Italian opera. In their own training, they often imperil their health by taking steroids and other drugs that, if abused, can cause death. Only a fanatical monomania can account for this.

And death in other forms happens in sports much more often than the casual observer imagines. A survey prepared for the American Football coaches association shows 891 deaths directly due to football at all levels from 1931-1983. (Most of these are at the high school level.) In the same time period, there were 465 deaths indirectly due to football for a total of 1358. By any score, this is a lot of deaths.

I do not contend that these statistics and analyses match the previous criteria for fanaticism. Certainly they are for the most part accidental, and not at all on a level with homicidal soccer hooligans. But some players deliberately set out to injure others, and sometimes are applauded by zealous coaches, parents, sportscasters, and audiences for doing so. Perhaps it needs to be rethought just what is involved in being a "fan."

CHAPTER 16, NOTES

1. I hasten to distinguish the form of wrestling popular on television with the legitimate sport, as practiced in the Olympic games.
2. "Riot Blamed on Tories," *Los Angeles Times*, 6 June 1985. Lang attributed soccer violence to "the kind of economic system Thatcher has created." It should be noted that "full employment" socialist societies have also seen rioting and death at athletic events. Some twenty people perished in violence at Moscow's Lenin Stadium in 1982. See Clive Gammon, "A Day of Horror and Shame" *Sports Illustrated*, 10 June 1985, 30. There was once a war between Honduras and El Salvador over a soccer game. See "The Soccer War" by Ryszard Kapuscinski, *Harpers*, June 1986, 47-55.
3. Alfie Kohn, "Soccer Riot: Competition is to Blame" *Los Angeles Times*, 5 June 1985. If, as Kohn contends, competition itself is to blame, why have there been no deaths at bowling, chess, or golf matches?

CHAPTER 17
THE THIN
GENERATION

> You'll love the new you.
> —from a weight reduction ad

There is a passage in Tom Clancy's technological thriller, *The Hunt For Red October*, in which some Russian submariner's joke about the way Americans like their women—blonde and thin. The Eastern Bloc *apparatchik* apparently prefers his female comrades a bit more beefy; a Hanna Mandlikova, say, over Christie Brinkley. Whether this information matches Clancy's other meticulous research for accuracy one cannot be sure, but it does not require a lot of insight to discover that thinness is one of the most rampant enthusiasms in recent memory.

Disarmament crusaders will doubtless find it distressing that many American women fear being fat more than they do nuclear war. This piece of data was discovered by professional psychologists and researchers, who broadcast their findings in the PBS documentary, "Thinness: The American Obsession" in January of 1985. These ladies would rather work their thighs into shape on Nautilus machines than participate in a "die in" over a Nautilus submarine. Perhaps an enterprising protester could combine the two activities: Push-ups for Peace.

Thinness propaganda is omnipresent. Every food, it seems, comes in a low-calorie version, even beer. A

particularly annoying California television commercial featured three wispy, cavorting adolescents sipping some taste-
less low-calorie gumbo while chirpy voices sang: "Skinny
girls, how do they do it? They drink the skinny girls' drink."
In an older version, an anatomically perfect woman nibbles
wafers and claims, "my shape belongs to Figurines."

Every shopping center has its "fitness center" full of
clanging exercise machines, damp bodies, and loud, fast
music. Some of these centers are open around the clock; they
have replaced the singles bar as a social meeting place. These
are the *fanum*, the temples of thinness.

Tabloid newspapers in supermarkets feature full-page
ads of "miraculous" diets and potions, accompanied by before-
and-after photos showing the behemoth-to-ballerina trans-
formation, topped off with headlines like: I LOST 266
POUNDS IN SEVEN DAYS! Sparkling testimonies of a
changed attitude, increase in popularity and enhanced sex
life usually follow. In finer print at the bottom one sees:
These fantastic results can be yours, too! Here's how to
order.

Jane Fonda has perceived and exploited a radical shift
in the *angst* axis: in 1968 it was Vietnam; in 1985 it's trim
tummies and tight buttocks. Cher, Victoria Principal, and
other sirens of the screen, along with magazine cover icons
like Cheryl Tiegs, have marketed their own workout books.
Sweats and leotards are *de rigueur*. Aerobics videos and television exercise programs are thriving.

In all these trends, one notices that the Christian community differs little from the general populace. In some cases
it denounces the trend, then in short order proceeds to
sanitize and adopt it. Thus, instead of Jazzercise, we find
"Praisercise"; replacing *The Jane Fonda Workout Book* is a
program called "Firm Believer." Syndicated cartoonist Tim
Downs, a Christian, has lampooned these imitations. Chuck
Laylo, one of his characters, proposes an exercise idea called,
"A Mighty Fortress is My Bod."

But what is going on here? One can applaud the popular desire for physical fitness, but does this have to do with health or appearance? The evidence suggests the latter.

A model interviewed on the PBS "Thinness" documentary pointed out how those who market glamor and/or thinness use the medium of photography to eliminate imperfections. The right poses, filters, and lenses, plus the judicious use of an airbrush add up to what this particular model called, "a fantasy." Indeed, the contrast between the glossy paper version of this woman and her actual persona was striking. They were different entities: a person and an image. A "look" is being sold—call it "Thinness Un-realism"—and there are many takers. For many, if not most, the fantasy is unattainable, and hence remains a kind of ex-clusive, physical gnosticism. A rule of fanaticism seems to be that the more unrealistic a goal, the more ardently it is pursued.

The use of religious language in this thinness cult— the word *miracle*, for instance—is not accidental. The pitch is very similar to "You must be born again," but contains a strong element of promise that runs something like this: "You'll love the new you!" Like sports, it very nearly reduces people to their bodies. A sleek profile is the object of devo-tion; pounds and ounces are its beatitudes; calories and flab its demons, and admiring looks are its blessings and rewards. It amounts to a total way of life.

Several women told the PBS documentarians that every act of eating became a conflict. Some would weigh themselves in the morning, and if they were so much as a half-pound above their goal, it would ruin their whole day. More extreme still, others took laxatives to shed pounds. All this is consistent with Hoffer's principle that when people attempt to save themselves, ("become the new you!") par-ticularly by chasing fantasies, fanaticism results. Some are deadly serious about it.

I believe the strange phenomenon of anorexia ner-vosa—the refusal to eat—is related to this in some cases. A very few women or girls would rather die than fail the exacting standards of the thinness cult. In a way, they are special cases, but in another way they typify us all. "I am who I am," says God; "I am not who I am," say too many of his creatures. God alone is satisfied with what he is; we all want to be, or appear to be, what we are not. And the sad anorexic women acting out their death wish are not alone in violating the homicide taboo with their own persons.

CHAPTER 18
DYING YOUNG

Now more than ever seems it rich to die
To cease upon the midnight with no pain

—Keats

Young people in the United States are killing themselves in record numbers. The traditionally high suicide rates of Japan and Sweden have been surpassed in America. The adolescent suicide rate has more than tripled since 1974 and is 33 percent higher than that of the general population. The 15-24 age group is the only segment of society whose death rate has increased in recent times. [1]

These kind of figures shock, like casualty lists from a war. What makes them particularly distressing is that none of this was supposed to happen. It was widely thought a generation ago that the youth of the 1980s would achieve unparalleled heights. The products of Bigger and Better Education, protected from the superstitions of the past, materially equipped, and emotionally "fulfilled," they were to become the new *ubermenschen*, a model for all time. Untold billions were, and are, spent to achieve this. All is poised for an outburst of "life-affirming" creativity. What we get in all too many cases is twanging guitars, alcoholism, eroticism, and a Gadarene rush to commit *sepuku*. [2]

Medical, psychological, and sociological explanations for suicide abound, but it is a mysterious subject, as in

Churchill's dictum on the Russians, hidden in a riddle and wrapped in an enigma. Studies of individual cases are necessarily post facto. Shakespeare called it "the question." Albert Camus referred to it as the only philosophical problem. Certainly no one denies that life and death issues are the province of religion. Nancy Kehoe, a psychologist and nun, asks, "Why, in the face of suicide, which is a person's ultimate statement about life and death, do we separate mental health and belief?"[3]

Perhaps we do this because professionals have made suicide the specialty of people who describe it like this: "Suicide is a biological, sociocultural, interpersonal, dyadic existential malaise."[4] It could be that psychiatrists who analyze suicide as, "strong cathexis of the self with superego aggressive energy and inadequate cathexis with narcissistic libido," frighten non-specialists away.[5]

In spite of the fact that more money and energy has been expended in the study of suicide in the past three decades than in the previous millennium, the rate continues to climb. The computer printout of literature on the subject weighs nearly six pounds[6] and is longer than a football field! Hence, there are good reasons for ignoring the standard explanations and seeing suicide in religious terms—as an act of fanaticism.

The pagan tradition held suicide as the most honorable form of death. John Donne's list of notable suicides in the ancient world runs to over three pages and includes Socrates, Seneca, Lucretius, Mithridates, and Hannibal. At Masada, Jewish zealots killed themselves rather than face capture and death at the hands of the Romans. While these were not acts of fanaticism, some of the actions of early Christians clearly were.

Although the church has always opposed suicide, in its early centuries there were instances of believers committing suicide, thinly disguised as martyrdom.[7] There is a certain logic to it: if we are really citizens of heaven, why not go there as soon as possible? Those who thought this way saw

Jesus' death as a kind of suicide. But Jesus' command to love one's neighbor as oneself is meaningless if suicide is permitted. God has also designated tasks for us in this world.

Are hunger strikers indulging in fanaticism or heroism? This depends entirely on one's view of the worth of their cause. Certainly the devotees of anything or anyone cannot go to much more of an extreme than this; unless of course they resort to killing other people instead of themselves, which is much more common than hunger strikes.

If these are examples of fanaticism, then it is the kind of fanaticism that sometimes elicits admiration, as in the case of Bobby Sands of the IRA, who starved himself to death several years ago to protest British policy in Northern Ireland. In similar style a would-be fanatic/hero—a leftist clergyman, for example—might want to torch himself in public over, say, the nuclear arms race, but backs off thinking that the Environmental Impact Statement might be tricky to procure. The true fanatic/hero goes all the way. Like Nechayev, it does not bother him that he is a doomed man.

In other cases, the question of fanaticism is not in doubt. The mass suicide rehearsed and carried out by the Rev. Jim Jones was performed in the name of an egalitarian socialist utopia, and has already been discussed earlier in this work.

The bizarre MOVE (the initials have no particular meaning) group in Philadelphia lived in a barricaded house full of rats and excrement. Eschewing technology and even baths, they nevertheless used loudspeakers to threaten neighbors, the President, and the police. They were a destructive, nihilistic group that found virtually everything in life offensive. They drew their solidarity from the notion that the world was against them, and, indeed, the world had many good reasons for this stance, most of them deliberately engendered by MOVE itself. A number of them died when police attempted to dislodge the group in May of 1985 (there had been violent confrontations before, in 1978).

Philadelphia mayor Wilson Goode called them terrorists, dedicated to destruction and desirous of a violent confrontation. Ron Javers of *Philadelphia Magazine* described MOVE's members as "on a death trip."[9] When the police attacked, MOVE cadres poured gasoline all through the house, surely a suicidal gesture. The fire quickly spread through the entire neighborhood. Like Samson, they probably wanted to see how many they could take with them.

And like MOVE, many young people are "on a death trip." In spite of the mountain of data that might contend otherwise, they kill themselves not because they are ill, but because they want to. Steve Bruno, who works with suicides in Phoenix, the city with the highest suicide rate, told me that some young people have romanticized death. They feel that just beyond the barrier is a peaceful world where they will be able to meet their departed friends yet still observe the earthly scene. Some popular rock groups cultivate this death imagery, which is often blatantly satanic.

Others do it as an act of defiance or a response to failure. In today's society with its multiplicity of trained counselors, therapists, support groups, etc., failure is difficult to handle. Failure against overwhelming odds is one thing; failure with vast resources on one's side is something else. People who fail under these conditions sometimes view suicide as the only promise they can keep, the only feat they can successfully pull off. But such people can be dangerous to others.

Phil Riccio, who works at a crisis center in Phoenix, told me that every suicide is potential homicide; that is, the suicidal person is very much capable of killing others instead of herself. Suicide can be an irrefutable "take that!" gesture, a way of gaining infallibility by having the ultimate "last word."

Much of this is still shrouded in mystery. But it is no mystery that the homicide taboo (which includes self-murder) is being broken *en masse*. This happens in spite of counseling, coddling, medical treatment, much theorizing, and even Christian teaching.[10] Wherever there are deaths of this magnitude, there is fanaticism. And there is a bizarre twist to this subject.

Not everyone sees the wild proliferation of suicide as an appalling trend. Groups that favor and facilitate suicide are appearing. The British-based EXIT (formerly the Voluntary Euthanasia Society) publishes *A Guide to Self-Deliverance*, which includes scores of ways to do yourself in with easily procured, legal materials. With apologies to Walker Percy, this, not *Lost in the Cosmos*, is the last self-help book a person will ever need. Notice the blatantly religious language—"deliverance"—in the title as a euphemism for murder or death.

Robert Kastenbaum, former president of the AAS, the American Association of Suicidologists, has said: "Suicide will gradually become the culturally sanctioned mode of death."[11] From this point, it is a short step to someone else— say, a future governmental "Quality of Life Arbitrator"—deciding who shall live, and who shall not.[12] If suicide trends and facilitation continue unopposed and unabated, some future political True Fanatic will find a wealth of received ideas at his disposal for destructive ends.

CHAPTER 18, NOTES
1. Lloyd Billingsley, "Half in Love with Easeful Death," *Eternity*, March 1985, 28.
2. Japanese word for suicide.
3. George Howe Colt, "Suicide," *Harvard Magazine*, September- October 1983, 59.
4. Ibid., 49.
5. Ibid., 62.
6. Ibid., p. 49. 7. Billingsley, 31.
8. Matthew 22:39.
9. Quoted in John J. Goldman, "Move's Philosophy: Militant Blend of Anti-Materialism, Contradiction," *Los Angeles Times*, 15 May 1985, 11.
10. Specialists I talked to claim that just as many young people from Christian backgrounds attempt suicide as any other group.
11. Colt, 63.
12. This, in fact, already happens. Some doctors apply a formula to handicapped infants to determine their "quality of life." QL (quality of life) = NE (natural endowments) x H + S (home and society.)

CHAPTER 19
BEING PROPHETIC: THE UNILATERAL DEATH-WISH

> He was one of those Idealists who, once struck by some over-whelming idea, becomes obsessed by it, sometimes for the rest of his life. He cannot ever really grasp it, but he believes it passionately, and his life becomes an uninterrupted series of agonizing pangs, as if he were half-crushed by a heavy stone.
>
> —Dostoyevsky, from *The Possessed*

One idea calculated to make a future or current True Fanatic salivate is the popular dogma that The World Must Come To An End Soon. This is not a reference to those theological expositors preoccupied with the details of eschatology. More and more, these people—dispensationalists like John Walvoord for example— say that they don't know when prophetic events will take place. Jesus Christ himself said as much.[1] Some modern pundits who see themselves as "prophetic" are more certain of matters.

The current "peace" movement in Europe and North America has something in common with the Munster commune already dealt with in this book. They are both millenarian phenomena, that is, certain that apocalyptic events are on the horizon, and that specific kinds of activism are therefore necessary.

For some reason, human beings treat a chronological non-event such as the end of a millennium, a century, or even a decade as something of startling significance. John of

Leiden and his merry band of Anabaptist fanatics, for example, derived support from the fact that their antics coincided with the fifteen hundredth anniversary of the death of Christ, give or take a few years (they were prophets, not mathematicians). It was, as carpenters often say, "close enough."

In less than fifteen years, history's odometer will flip over to A.D. 2000. This is enough in itself to stir utopians into apocalyptic prognostications. In 1979, pacifism and poverty promoter Ron Sider saw the chances for nuclear war, "in the next 20 years" as "50-50."[2] How did he know? "Responsible scientists" and "people in Washington" said so. One is immediately struck by the authoritarianism of this. One does not want to base one's actions on what scientists and people in Washington say.

Sider's baleful tome, *Nuclear Holocaust and Christian Hope*, set out a number of gory scenarios. Jonathan Schell's *Fate of the Earth* similarly implied that unless we had world government by next Tuesday, we'd all be ashes. Other doom-gloom prophets are now well-financed and equipped with Panavision movie cameras, producing such maudlin, didactic fare as *The Day After* and *Threads*.

These, along with the strident, incessant rhetoric that accompanies them, are designed to frighten the living innards out of everyone, especially children. They say with the voice of revelation: *This is what is going to happen*. The terrified audience becomes so freighted with scenes of carnage and destruction that they ask: "What can we do?" They are told in so many words that they are most guilty for heretofore having done nothing. This is the same technique used by some television and radio preachers. They create a little guilt, implant some troubling thoughts, then imply that all can be solved by mailing in a donation. Anti-Nuclear prophets, secular and Christian, grab their audience by the lapels and shout into their faces until they are guilt-stricken, trembling, and incoherent, then trot out their remedy:

unilateral disarmament by the United States and the West. Activism to promote this is demanded.

One small consolation is that in the past, promoters of this position would deny that unilateral disarmament (by the United States, of course) is what they meant; they now come out for it openly. Jim Wallis of *Sojourners* magazine calls for unilateral disarmament on the part of the United States.[3] The Rev. John Stott urges people to be nuclear pacifists,[4] which amounts to the same thing. Sider, in *Nuclear Holocaust*, urges complete pacifism.[5] Jacques Ellul has noted the suicidal, almost nihilistic strain in doctrine that the state should not employ force. "To say that the state should not employ force is simply to say that there should be no state."[6]

Malcolm Muggeridge has noted that this issue is not a question of hardware, but of heart. After Hiroshima, some of his own friends, perfectly sensible people, sold everything and ran off to await the nuclear Armageddon that they, like Ron Sider now, thought was inevitable and imminent. Muggeridge commented that the introduction of powerful new weapons altered nothing, since it was the will to destroy that mattered, not the means.[7]

Dean Curry of Messiah College also challenges those who demonize weapons themselves.[8] It is the *intention* of those who possess nuclear weapons that counts, not the mere existence of these weapons. Why does the United States not enter into nuclear arms reduction talks with the French or British? Because these nations, though nuclear-armed, harbor no malevolent intentions toward the United States.

What unilateral disarmament by the United States would do would be to make nuclear war more, not less, likely. The Dictatorship of the Proletariat of the USSR see themselves not as politicians, but the Incarnations of the Will of History. History, in their view, has determined that they will win. The "enemy class" (the West) will be vanquished. What a handy job for nuclear weapons, especially if they could be used with impunity, which would happen in the case of nuclear disarmament by the West.

We have already cited peace crusader Wolf Biermann to the effect that the Soviets would strike immediately if they felt they could get away with it. But Biermann also provides a classic example of death-wishing fanaticism. Knowing the true nature and intentions of the Soviet dictators, he nevertheless says: "Therefore I advocate unilateral disarmament wherever I go. It's time for some life-saving illogic."[9] Michael Greve, who is quoting Biermann, offers this comment:

> Biermann is a poet, and one should not hold such irresponsibility against him too much. Indeed, perhaps he deserves gratitude for expressing the program of the peace movement in a single sentence—a call for an end to reason. [10]

To link this subject with the previous chapter on suicide, students at various American universities have demanded that the school administration provide suicide pills to be used in the event of nuclear war. This is fanaticism, an act perpetrated by the superstition that a nuclear war is inevitable. Other students with clearer heads have objected to "the pill" on the grounds that such a war is not inevitable.

The unilateralists would doubtless rather not take such measures. They would rather be Red than dead. Joseph Brodsky, an emigre Russian poet who would rather be free than Red, points out that if disarmament advocates have their way, this question is irrelevant.

> As for those members of the public who ponder the advantages of being Red rather than dead, they had better be notified that their calculations are premature: it is the Reds who will decide whether they are to become Red or fall dead. [11]

One notes of the unilateralists, especially the Christians, that they make disarmament *the* issue. During the 1984 presidential campaign, Jim Wallis and liberal pro-Mondale clergy falsely accused president Reagan of "Armageddon theology."[12] Ironically, these unilateralists, with their mania for the subject, and who hold it as dogma that a war is coming, are the true Armageddon theologians. They fit Churchill's definition of a fanatic as one who can't change his mind and won't change the subject. There is a reason for this.

It is called "speaking prophetically" and was best described in its popular form by Kenneth A. Myers of *Eternity* magazine:

> Calling yourself prophetic is certainly a useful rhetorical device. You assume the moral high ground and remove the issue at hand from the arena of debate and discussion. While you make declamations with broad and passionate flourishes, anyone who disagrees with you has the unattractive task of responding with facts and analyses. You look heroic; they look like a pack of accountants, or the Inquisition.[13]

No Soviet ruler, to my knowledge, has ever admitted error. Indeed, totalitarian socialism depends on the perception that the Dictatorship of the Proletariat is infallible. Similarly, "prophetic" pronouncements on nuclear arms are, as Myers points out, set forth at high decibels as being the *only* view, the divine view, in the same sense as the Old Testament prophets.[14] But speaking prophetically—especially when one is taken seriously, as Wallis and Sider are—involves some baggage that, all too often, is ignored.

Speaking prophetically means, in effect, that if you retract the prophetic statements or change your mind, your whole prophetic posture can be perceived as only so much balloon juice—a fraud. The prophetic speaker, like Soviet officials or the Ayatollah Khomeini, is locked into his stance. Monomania, which may be another word for fanaticism, is the result. We have previously noted that infallibility is the *force de frappe* in the fanatic's armory. Add a dash of utopianism[15] and mayhem may follow.

The real danger posed by fanatics is that they should gain a following—something they are very good at—and be

taken seriously by the populace and especially the government. The likelihood is small, but this may happen with the
issue of unilateral disarmament. In which case, oblivion,
please.

CHAPTER 19, NOTES

1. Mark 13:32.
2. An interview with Ron Sider, *The Wittenburg Door*, October- November, 1979, 16.
3. Jim Wallis, quoted in an interview in "The Christian as Citizen: Three Views," *Christianity Today*, 19 April 1985, 27.
4. See the cover blurbs on *Nuclear Holocaust and Christian Hope*.
5. See "Defending the United States by Nonmilitary Means," in *Nuclear Holocaust and Christian Hope* (Downer's Grove: InterVarsity Press, 1983), 273-92. In the event of a Soviet invasion, Sider advocates telling the arrivals that "troops will be welcome as tourists but will be opposed as invaders." Space does not permit a treatment, but the whole section is a piece of fantasy, to my knowledge unparalleled in all of literature, fiction or non-fiction. Practically, the strategy would simply be to hand over millions of innocent people to be slaughtered. Far from being heroes, high-profile pacifists would be helping the invaders to find and punish those who would surely take up arms in resistance.
6. Jacques Ellul, *The Political Illusion* (New York: Vintage Books, 1972), 76.
7. Malcolm Muggeridge, *Chronicles of Wasted Time*, 2 (New York: Morrow, 1974): 264.
8. Dean Curry, "Terrible Weapons, Seductive Illusions," *Eternity*, March, 1985, 19-22.
9. Michael Greve, "Green Fungus," *National Review*, 28 December 1984, 25.
10. Ibid.
11. Joseph Brodsky, "Disarmament Disillusions," *Harpers*, February, 1985, 24.
12. Armageddon Theology is the belief that the Bible's prophetic scheme includes a nuclear war.
13. Ken Myers, "Truth and the Prophet Motive," *Eternity*, 5 May 1985, 11.
14. Read carefully the interview with Ron Sider in *The Wittenburg Door*, October-November, 1979. Sider never acknowledges that there are other positions on the subject other than his own.
15. Since nuclear power and nuclear weapons cannot be "uninvented," all talk of abolishing them is completely unrealistic, as is the notion of total disarmament. This is truly "utopian" since it has never happened. There is precedent, on the other hand, for arms reduction, a much more realistic expectation.

CHAPTER 20
FANATICISM, FASCISM, RACISM

"You're damn right I'm teaching violence."
—William Potter Gale

Fascist and fascism[1] are two words misused with regularity. Toward the end of his life, George Orwell complained that the only remaining use for fascist was "something that one doesn't like." Orwell saw, correctly, that fascism was a revolutionary mass movement[2] with a nationalist dimension. Fascism is national socialism, for which the abbreviation "Nazi" stands.

Orwell's contemporary, Evelyn Waugh, also complained about this sort of abuse, particularly from leftists who described everything from fox-hunting to petty theft to Catholicism as "Fascist."[3] Had Waugh lived until today he might be surprised to find a fellow Christian calling those without an appropriate level of enthusiasm for the Sanctuary Movement, "Christian Fascists."[4]

Fascism in its true sense as a mass movement was nearly moribund in the England of 1938. Waugh pointed out, however, that it did carry on as, "a form of anti-Semitism."[5] This is the key to current manifestations of fascism.[6]

Neo-nazism in North America is narrow on political theory but wide on hatred of Jews and blacks. It is preoccupied with the sadistic trappings, dark symbolism, and violent methodology of nazism, not its materialist philosophical base, derived largely from Nietzsche.

The various groups involved—the Aryan Nations, the Ku Klux Klan, the Posse Comitatus, the American Nazi Party and other groups—are remarkably similar, though they have their doctrinal differences. Neo-nazism's sustaining superstitions are the myths of racial superiority and the notion of a Jewish conspiracy that rules the world. Such fictions have existed for centuries but were given shape in the fraudulent *Protocols of the Elders of Zion*, used by German Nazis as justification for their persecution of Jews.[7]

The racial hierarchy so prevalent among these groups is sometimes given a biblical gloss. For example, Jesus is held not to be a Jew, but of Germanic stock, making white Aryans, not Jews, the chosen people of God.[8] Blacks, Hispanics and other minorities are considered soulless, "mongrel peoples."[9] The Fascist eschatology bears striking similarities to Charles Manson's vision of an impending race war. Details may be sketchy, but the neo-Nazis are certain that a lot of people must die. They then attempt by their actions to fulfill their own prophecy. This is a sure recipe for fanaticism.

William Potter Gale operates the Ministry of Christ Church in Mariposa, California. Like another racist, anti-Semitic group, the Church of Jesus Christ Christian, Gale has given his hateful vision a Christian vocabulary. But this sort of thing has about as much relation to Christianity as the Sermon on the Mount does to *Mein Kampf*. Gale is remarkably candid. In early 1983, he broadcast over KTTL-FM in Dodge City, "You're damn right I'm teaching violence. It's about time somebody is telling you to get violent, whitey."[10]

That these groups are fanatical and dangerous cannot be denied. They have cached large amounts of weapons, and shown themselves to be more than willing to break the homicide taboo in quest of their "resurrection of society." Their racial hatred is a way of salvaging their stunted, insecure selves; their violent, revolutionary machinations are their way of saving the world. Some, like Ku Klux Klansman

Tom Metzger, have tried the electoral process. Metzger ran for congress in California's forty-third district in 1980. He was soundly thumped; but that he got any votes at all is alarming.[11] This loss probably served as confirmation to his soul mates than violence is the true way to personal and national salvation.

These groups, of course, are also present in Europe. In the sixties, Malcolm Muggeridge, writing in the *New Statesman*, condemned anti-Semitism. For this act, a group called the Anti-Jewish Pogrom Committee of the People's Liberation Army pronounced upon him a sentence of death.[12] It was never carried out.

Claire Sterling describes the bombing of the railway station at Bologna by Neo-Nazis. Eighty-four people died. It was the worst terrorist act in Europe since the last war.[13] All moral people the world over will rightly loathe and resist the actions and recruiting overtures of these groups.

But while these right-wing terrorist fanatics are as dangerous and anti-democratic as any group can be, it would be a mistake to build them into too big of a bogey, as the electronic media have sometimes done. A California law officer who requested anonymity estimated the following of William Potter Gale as under forty persons, possibly as low as ten or twelve.[14]

In the thirties, Waugh pointed out the dangers of excessive demonizing. When this is incessantly done, he wrote, the bogey may become real, and then, "we shall all lose by such a development."[15] The True Fanatic seeks publicity by his acts. He revels in coverage on the evening news, and gains status when interviewed.[16] If racist, anti-Semitic fanaticism is thus fueled by the gift of a free nationwide television audience, what Waugh wrote may be applied to us: we will all lose. (One should hasten to add here that racial hatred and anti-Semitism are no respecters of persons or races.)[17]

But that we are dealing with classic fanaticism cannot be doubted for a moment. Lenin's mentor Sergey Nechayev pronounced himself a "doomed man" at the beginning of his career. Hear Robert Jay Matthews, an American Neo-Nazi, exhort his fellows:

> Give your soul to God and pick up your gun,
> It is time to deal in lead;
> We are the legions of the damned,
> The Army of the Already Dead.[18]

CHAPTER 20, NOTES

1. The word derives from *fasces*, a bundle of rods enclosing an axe, with the blade protruding. It was a symbol of power in ancient Rome.
2. Bernard Crick, *George Orwell: A Life* (London: Secker and Warburg, 1981), 192.
3. Evelyn Waugh, *The Essays, Articles and Reviews of Evelyn Waugh* (Boston: Little, Brown, 1984), 223.
4. Daniel Ritchie, "Sanctuary," *Eternity*, June, 1985, 33.
5. Waugh, 223.
6. This writer once covered a Ku Klux Klan rally for a Spanish language paper. I didn't quite know what to make of it all at the time. A fellow journalist asserted, "this is fascism." She was right.
7. See Hannah Arendt's *The Origins of Totalitarianism* (New York: Harcourt, Brace, Jovanovich, 1966).
8. John Snell, "FBI Probes Church With Racist Beliefs" *The Oregonian*, 5 May 1985.
9. Ibid. In basing good/bad distinctions on race, these white supremacists, in spite of their religious talk, show themselves true materialists. See James Burtchaell, *Rachel Weeping* (New York: Harper and Row, 1982), 141-239, for a discussion of racial superiority theories and their consequences.
10. Ibid.
11. Metzger ran against Rep. Claire Burgener, a Republican, and received 35,107 votes to Burgener's 253,949.
12. Ian Hunter, *Malcolm Muggeridge: A Life* (Nashville: Thomas Nelson, 1980), 214.
13. Claire Sterling, *The Terror Network* (New York: Holt, Rinehart and Winston, 1981), 1.
14. Snell, "FBI Probes."
15. Waugh, 223.
16. Ernst Zundel, prosecuted in Canada for distributing hate literature, gained much free publicity for his anti-Semitic theories in the ensuing trial. See Donald Coxe, "Return of the Big Lie" *National Review*, 31 May 1985, 36.
17. David Anderson of United Press International, interviewed in *The Wittenburg Door*, December 1983-January 1984, 18, refers to Reverend Louis Farrakhan as a leader who could be "very important" in a positive sense. Farrakhan makes no secret of his anti-Jewish prejudices, and has called Judaism a "gutter religion" (See "Democrats Must Renounce Farrakhan," *San Diego Tribune*, 28 June 1984). Jesse Jackson, who aspires to be President, referred to New York as "Hymietown," leading liberal commentator Tom Braden to call Jackson an anti-Semite. See "This Week" *National Review*, 3 May 1985, 14.
18. Quoted by Kitty Caparella, in "Days Numbered for FBI's Neo-Nazi Insider," *The Oregonian*, 18 April 1985.

CHAPTER 21
DANSE MACABRE

Everything has limits, except human stupidity.
　　　　　　　　　　　　　　　　—German Proverb

Michael Straight, former vice chairman of the National Endowment for the Arts, received an application for funds expressed as follows:

> I will rent a ground level studio with high ceilings and a cement floor, adjacent to a lush meadow. And to this place I will bring some friends and some strangers. I will bring Pigme, a full grown sow (whom I have known since her ninth day), two female rabbits (who know each other and me), a buck (stranger), two ringed neck doves (strangers), a woolly monkey, Georgina (who knows me slightly), a cat, Blackflash (who knows me), a young boy, Brett (who knows me and the two female rabbits), and a young girl, Lavina (who knows me and Brett slightly). We will all move in together.[1]

This was all described as "environmental art with social utility." Its "creator" also requested funds for video equipment and a motorbike. And, yes, it was funded. Another example of your tax dollars at work in the cause of Art. (One wonders how Pigme got along with the doves and the cat. Did Lavina find Georgina congenial? Did the female rabbits decamp in search of mates? Who made the beds and did the dishes? Most of all, how did the critics assess it?)

In this utilitarian age, things are judged by how they

best serve society, not for any intrinsic beauty or value they might have. Those who bail the public trough for grants subscribe to the notion that art can help resolve social problems, "bring people together," or even make us "better people." In short, Art is given a redemptive value, a religious status. And if what passes for art does all these wonderful things, it follows that the government should fund as much of it as possible. Hence, as Hoffer observed, an eruption of fanaticism in the arts.

The examples are numerous: laundry strung across rivers; Macbeth shortened to fifteen minutes and performed on roller skates (Lady Macbeth rides a moped). The latter gem was funded by the good people at the Salt Lake Council for the arts. These examples qualify due to sheer outrageousness. They are a result of another sort of fanaticism: the pursuit of salvation through personal experience, in this case embodied in fraudulent non- art.

And it is not just government officials and those who milk them who will now call anything "art." Some of the world's leading "experts" have experienced serious lapses. In Livorno, Italy, last year, three college students saw divers searching for some unfinished heads that sculptor Amedeo Modigliani (1884-1920) reportedly threw into a canal. In a few hours the students carved a head of their own out of an old chunk of sidewalk. They then plastered their creation with grass and pitched it into the canal, where several days later it was discovered.[2]

Giulio Carlo Argan, a prominent art historian and former mayor of Rome, pronounced the work "authentic." Another famous critic, Cesare Brandi, wrote, "in these two scabrous stones there is the Annunciation, there is the Presence." Enzo Carol, curator of a Modigliani show, announced, "These stones have a soul."

The students, none of whom was an artist, expected their fraud to be discovered, but when the critics began their hallelujahs, they went public with the claim that they had carved the head, producing photos to prove it.

As might be imagined, there was a great furor over this, including charges that the youths had been put up to the stunt by their parents in order to embarrass the mayor of Livorno, a Communist. One critic stubbornly maintained that the head was authentic and challenged the students to produce another one, this time on television. To the chagrin of the expert, the three youths proceeded to do this, in front of a national television audience, to the utter humiliation of the art gurus. It was as though a highbrow New York critic had hailed *Porky's* as the greatest film of the century.

The incident serves as a parable for the fact that much modern art cannot speak for itself, but must be interpreted by the Art Clergy as to its value, and, of course, social and personal utility.

And there is a lesson here, too. Pietro Ferucci, one of the students, stated that from that point on, he would make up his own mind about what was art.

In this utilitarian age, art is practically synonymous with "creativity." There need not be any modern version of, say, *War and Peace*, the Sistine Chapel, or *Missa solemnis*. No, the mere intention to produce art is enough—at least to get the project funded.

As C.S. Lewis pointed out, human beings can only absorb, reflect, and rearrange. They cannot create in the sense that God does:

> If I read the New Testament aright, it leaves no room for "creativeness" even in a modified or metaphorical sense. Our whole destiny seems to lie in the opposite direction . . . in acquiring a fragrance that is not our own but borrowed, in becoming clean mirrors filled with the image of a face that is not ours.[3]

Malcolm Muggeridge, a man many consider to be the finest living writer of the English language, professes to know nothing about what is called "creative writing." During a brief stint at a Canadian university, he insisted that he not be asked to teach it.[4]

Paul Vitz comments that "creativity" in current usage,

is simply "a gift from the self to the self." As proof of this, he cites a lecturer who argued for "creative masturbation."[5]

Of course, it is not just the public-funded art that abides by this "creative principle." The private sector, particularly the record business, leads the way. Serious jazz musicians claim, rightly, that media awards programs pay more attention to "freak shows," and whether a singer's hair a given night happens to be orange or green. Rock concerts often have little to do with music. They are "life affirming celebrations"; in short, religious experiences.

Like the Italian experts so ready to find "soul" in a hacked up chunk of sandstone, many music critics are nothing more than cheerleaders for fanaticism. Prince, who sings about incest and mimes masturbation on stage, is described as "transforming inner turmoil into galvanizing rock spectacle." Sample this creative hagiography:

> Once the mainstream audience got a load of this seductive sexual renegade and his state-of-the-heart neo-gospel electro-funk music, it didn't take long for them to join the core following that had been with him all along.[6]

Furthermore, one song was a "hyped-up benediction," and the sexual renegade and his electro-funk neo-gospel service were not through yet.

> All of a sudden we were part of a crisis-of-conscience psychodrama as Prince teased and flirted with the audience, struggled with temptation, looked heavenward and talked to an angry God, blamed us for making him bad, and comtemplated the nature of love and lust and of life and death.[7]

It was all, the witness testified, an "apocalyptic morality play."

This kind of criticism may be found in any newspaper, or even middle-brow magazines like Newsweek and Time, the cover of which is post-Christendom's most notable stained-glass window. Peering from this window recently was Madonna, a singer who mimes oral sex on stage.

What it all amounts to is hermeneutics, a self-proclaimed member of the Art Clergy interpreting a musical freak/sex/noise show for confused Youth In Search of Salvation. And when "fans" are willing to trample their peers to death in a rush for the best seats, fanaticism of a more serious sort is in operation.

CHAPTER 21, NOTES

1. Ronald Berman, "The New Problem of Paying for Art," *Chronicles of Culture*, April, 1985, 19.

2. Amos Elon, "A Hoax that Embarrassed the Experts," *Parade*, 3 February 1985, 12-14.

3. C.S. Lewis "Christianity and Literature," in *Christian Reflections*, ed. Walter Hooper (Grand Rapids: Eerdmans, 1967), 6f.

4. Ian Hunter, *Malcolm Muggeridge: A life* (Nashville: Thomas Nelson, 1980), 216.

5. Paul Vitz, *Psychology as Religion: The Cult of Self-Worship* (Grand Rapids: Eerdmans, 1977), 63.

6. Richard Cromelin, "For Prince's Concert," *Los Angeles Times*, 20 February 1985.

7. Ibid.

CHAPTER 22
SELF-HELP RELIGION

There's only one son of god, and that's you, so it's time for
peace.   Reverend Terry Cole-Whittaker

One finds an abundance of material when searching
the religious scene for examples of fanaticism. The Hindus
used to incinerate widows on the funeral pyres of their husbands. The practice was called *suttee* and was banned by the
British, over furious Hindu objection, in the 1800s. The
practice of Hindu husbands murdering ("abetting suicide" is
how it is sometimes described) their wives in order to exact a
second dowry from another woman still carries on. [1]

On the American scene, there are eight members of a
Kentucky family who reportedly "received a divine com-
mand to make a human sacrifice," and ritually murdered
Mrs. Lucinda Mills, age seventy-two. [2]

A man named Bryan Stanley recently murdered a priest
and two other people because girls were allowed to read from
the Bible at a Mass. [3]

An undated Evangelical Press report in *Horizon International* magazine cites a fringe group within the Watch-
tower Society (Jehovah's Witnesses) as believing that singer
Michael Jackson is the returned Christ.

Several years ago, an Australian Christian attempted
to blow up the Mosque of Omar, in the belief that this would
speed up the fulfillment of prophecy.

Imported holy man Swami Rajneesh recruited throngs of American youth and took over a whole town in Oregon.

The Children of God, descendants of the early "Jesus People," and once of more or less orthodox Christian belief, now distribute pornography and practice incest. Children of God leader Moses David (Dave Berg) is reported to be living in Libya. If true, this is another confirmation that fanatics are all of a breed, irrespective of doctrine.

Where mysticism and quietism once dominated the religious scene, activism now predominates, providing fanatics fertile territory. One can applaud efforts against the terrible abortion holocaust, but when religious groups take to bombing clinics, they too disregard the homicide taboo. It matters not that, as of this writing, no one has been killed. These bombings are perpetrated in the belief that they will stop abortions. They will, of course, do nothing of the kind, but only provide abortionists with martyr status and more favorable television coverage. The bombings are acts of fanaticism.

The standard practices that elicit cries of "religious fanaticism" also deserve mention: spurious healing services, snake-handling in church; wild, out of order glossolalia;[4] bombastic, heavy-handed fundraising.

One could easily go on multiplying such examples. But to return to the Hoffer principle, it is when people do their own soul-saving that fanaticism occurs. Many of the worst excesses of self-salvation, self-motivation, and money-worship are now being given a liturgical expression as a formal religion. Until very recently, when she gave up her "religion" to pursue a straightforward message of "positive thinking," leading the way in this movement was the Rev. Terry Cole-Whittaker of La Jolla, California. She received national acclaim in *Newsweek* as a minister to careerist "yuppies," and as such probably represents the shape of things to come. A study of her and her former ministry presents a parable of contemporary self-fanaticism that fits Hoffer's definition perfectly.

"I call myself an Evangelistic, Pentecostal, Metaphysical Space Cadet," said Cole-Whittaker. "I'm not really Science of the Mind, I'm not a woman, I am spirit—birthless, deathless—I am cosmic."[5] Such a description requires no additional comment. And the creed of this birthless, deathless, not-a-woman Pentecostal space cadet?

At a service I attended in December of 1984, Reverend Terry said, "There's only one son of God and that's you, so it's time for peace." It also follows that if we are all gods, then our service should be directed toward ourselves. One is reminded of the psychotic Earl of Gurney in Peter Barnes's play, The Ruling Class. This earl, named Jack, gambolled about claiming to be God. When challenged as to how he knew he was God, he replied that when he prayed to God, he discovered he was talking to himself. One suspects that the Reverend Terry's theory of prayer ran more or less along the same lines.

At the same service, Reverend Terry added: "Why shouldn't you be the wealthiest person in the world, and everybody else just as wealthy as you?" This is like Andy Warhol's dictum that everyone should be famous for fifteen minutes. It remains to be seen how one can be the wealthiest person in the world if everyone else is just as wealthy; logical problems do not appear to be an obstacle for this brand of religion. But Reverend Terry is positively lucid on other points.

"You can have exactly what you want," she said, "when you want it, all the time. To get what you want, you have to go for it."[6] Reverend Terry explained in her sermon how she "goes for it." Unable to decide on a dessert at a restaurant, she ordered them all and took a bite out of each.

She apparently takes something of the same approach with husbands: she has had four, and is in the process of "mastering relationships." Asked who she would cast in a movie of her life story, she named Jessica Lange to play herself, Robert Wagner to play her first husband and Mickey Rooney to play the second. She wouldn't name the lucky actor to play the third, but "for the role of my fourth husband I would choose the Pope."[7] This is a film I would like to see.

Probing the literature of Reverend Terry's ministry, one notices a goulash of all sorts of remedies designed to promote health and happiness. Self-help books like *Your Erroneous Zones* abound, as do works on Eastern mysticism and prosperity tomes by writers like Reverend Ike.

In the brochure section there was a notice promoting "Deep Body Work," a massage technique designed to "free trapped patterns of energy." Also featured was "Group Rebirthing" which appeared to be a kind of breathing exercise. Applicants for this activity had to sign a release freeing Reverend Terry's ministries from responsibility if the participant was injured.

The church bulletin contained a notice of a "Dressing to Win" seminar. The right clothes, the right look, this implied, will guarantee success. The seminar was available for a few hundred dollars. In fact, all the church activities, even the Christmas banquet, cost money. The price of admission for the latter was $150. Parishioners were even invited to travel to India with Reverend Terry for a paltry $3,000. The $500 registration fee was non-refundable.

And there was something for everyone here. Those opposed to the arms race were invited to "Boogie for Peace." Admission was $35. Furthermore, there was an "Animal Ministry" that prayed for sick pets.

And on it goes *ad absurdum*. One can obviously have a good time describing all this, but there is a kind of pall hanging over it all. What these people seem fanatically set on doing is handing over their money in large amounts. Why would they do so if they did not believe that the purchased activities would bring some sort of fulfillment and happiness? This constitutionally mandated pursuit of happiness, as religiously defined by Reverend Terry and her many soul mates and imitators, will lead only to boredom and frustration. There is no amount of money, career, diet, exercise, or current religious leader under heaven, named among men, whereby we may either be saved or enjoy earthly bliss. The salvation comes from elsewhere; the bliss is an illusion. What kind of fanaticism will these people display when they find themselves sated and disgusted? Will the next wave of suicides be middle-aged burnouts instead of adolescents?

Since we have had some fun at Reverend Terry's expense, it is perhaps fair to conclude on a note of hope. Self-help salvation may turn out to be a form of pre-evangelism. Paul Vitz of New York University wrote a remarkable book about the cult of self-worship. He ended it thus:

> In another ten years millions of people will be bored with the cult of the self and looking for a new life. The uncertainty is not the existence of this coming wave of returning prodigals, but whether their Father's house, the true faith, will still be there to welcome and celebrate their return.[8]

CHAPTER 22, NOTES
 1. See Wendy Lozano, "India's Burning of Young Brides," *Los Angeles Times*, 16 January 1985.
 2. Ronald Knox, *Enthusiasm* (New York: Oxford, 1950), 582.
 3. "Man Upset by Girls' Reading of Bible at Mass Slays Priest, 2 Others," *Los Angeles Times*, 8 February 1985. Stanley identified himself as "Elijah" when apprehended by police. Fanatics seem to prefer Elijah over Moses or David.
 4. For an interesting perspective on glossolalia see "Some Vagaries of Revivalism" in Knox's *Enthusiasm*, particularly p. 553.
 5. Interview with Johnny Rogers entitled, "Terry Cole-Whittaker, When She Preaches, People Listen" in *Tuned In*, November 24-30, 1984, 3.
 6. Ibid., 2.
 7. Ibid., 6.
 8. Paul Vitz, *Psychology as Religion: The Cult of Self-Worship* (Grand Rapids: Eerdmans, 1977), 135.

CHAPTER 23
STATES' RITES

Homo politicus is by his very nature *homo religiosus*.
—Jacques Ellul

Paul Johnson points out in his masterful work, *Modern Times*, that what linked such people as Pol Pot, Mussolini, and Castro was, "their belief that politics was the cure for human ills."[1] The application of this principle has meant, as Johnson and anyone without ideological fungus on his retina can see, "poverty and death."[2]

And yet, the belief that statecraft is the cure for human ills is not confined to the distinguished gentlemen cited by Johnson. Since John Maynard Keynes, Roosevelt, and the New Deal, it has been a prevailing orthodoxy. Jacques Ellul comments:

> In the seventeenth century we could have written of the comic illusion. In our day the illusion has become tragic. It is political. People in our time, with even greater zeal than in the nineteenth century, invest political affairs with their passions and hopes, but live in a peculiarly distressing political trance.[3]

Those not caught in this trance, those who do not worship state social action, and, what is worse, who dare to suggest alternatives, are dubbed "reactionaries." These are the "true heretics"[4] of today, says Ellul, the French theologian and former Resistance fighter.

Malcolm Muggeridge once outraged the multitudes (by no means the only time or subject on which this has happened) by his comment that Mrs. Eleanor Roosevelt was a threat to freedom compared to which Adolph Hitler paled into insignificance.[5] It is the kind of statement I love: sweeping, opposed to all prevailing dogmas, apparently nonsensical, but on examination, glowing with a truth of its own. As Ian Hunter, Muggeridge's biographer, comments in defense of his subject, Hitler has been fought and vanquished; he is no longer a threat to freedom. But it remains to be seen if freedom "can survive the pernicious effects of New Deal liberalism."[6] This is very much an open question.

New Deal *realpolitik* is the notion that social problems are not individual, but "systemic," that is, "society's fault." Poverty and crime, the mythology goes, are the inevitable fallout of a free market economy and an open society. Given that the problem is systemic, the solution must be as well. Hence the State must function as a kind of omnipresent wet nurse, attending to the needs of every citizen. And the list of needs grows longer all the time. The State must solve all problems; in short, it must be our savior.

Other fundamentals of the political myth are: that free enterprise is antiquated, that profit is evil and "obscene," that those who achieve do so by exploiting others, and that wealth must be redistributed. The all-encompassing state, of course, is best qualified to do the latter activity.

Those who hold these doctrines often call themselves social democrats. They have held sway in England for some time; long enough in fact, for a detailed report card to be issued on whether their schemes do, in fact, work. They do not. The state as savior is a failure.

As R. Emmett Tyrrell Jr. points out in *The Future That Doesn't Work*, the plunge of Britain into demoralization, unemployment, and bankruptcy was "one of the most accurately and noisily predicted declines in world history."[7] Yet, social democrats still stridently pursue and advocate their superstitions. They hurl hackneyed pejoratives—"Thatcherism," "Reaganism"—at the concepts of individual responsibility and free markets.

In the United States, there is not only a growing body of evidence that American state-as-social-savior programs have failed, but that they have made the situation worse.

To fully examine the details would require an entire book, but it seems a fairly simple observation that one gets what one subsidizes. When the government subsidizes tobacco farmers, more tobacco will be forthcoming. If a government subsidizes poverty, it will get poverty; if it subsidizes abortions, it will get abortions. If it provides incentives for people to break up their families and not seek jobs, then people will do so.

This fits well with the spiritual vacuum of an age in which many have become moral eunuchs. As Ellul so aptly expresses it: "Because I am incapable of doing good in my own life, the state must do it in my place, by proxy."[8] Advertisers know all too well that human nature is to take the "easy" way.

It is worth noting how hesitant people are to even examine the evidence of welfare state failure. Charles Murray's *Losing Ground: American Social Policy, 1950-1980* is the most ambitious attempt to prove that governmental social action has created poverty, even though its intention was to eradicate it. Murray does not merely theorize, he uses hard data. James Skillen, reviewing this book in *Christianity Today*,[9] leaves the data questions "for others" when it would seem that the empirical side of the issue is the most important. He makes no attempt at all to answer the question, "What do the facts say?" Rather, he then proceeds to introduce a series of unanswered "Why?" questions that confuse the issue and avoid the book's thesis. Two other scholars, Ronald Nash and Jim Halteman, put in their yea and nay on the book (with the nay given priority), but coupled with the negative review, the overall effect is that Murray is outnumbered two to one. The title of the whole exchange is, *In Search of Something that Works*. In other words: Yes, current government programs have been a disaster, but there must be *some* government strategy that will work. Skillen's review implies that the task is to find this elusive strategy and support it, and above all disregard Murray's strategy that government welfare programs be scrapped.

This might seem like too much to make of a book review, but it shows that Ellul's political "illusion" remains "in the mind of those who believe they can modify reality in itself by political power."[10] Christians, of all people, should realize that:

> politics absolutely cannot deal with man's personal problems, such as good and evil, or the meaning of life, or the responsibilities of freedom.[11]

What Malcolm Muggeridge wrote in 1949 is true of many influential Christians today:

> In the public mind there was now a complete confusion between the Welfare State and the Christian religion, though, in point of fact, the two had very little connection with one another.[12]

That the state, through higher taxes, vast bureaucracies, and social spending, can achieve a better life for the poor, or, what is sometimes claimed, eradicate poverty altogether, is a superstition. So is the notion that something can be done by a government for vast numbers of people at no cost to those people themselves, or to the public in general. A hard look at the evidence of social destruction caused by government, coupled with a reading of the bitter outpourings of neo-socialist barkers like Tip O'Neill in *The Congressional Record* will confirm that activated superstition is indeed fanaticism.

Lyndon Johnson's "War on Poverty" was a more shocking defeat for the United States than Vietnam. And after every war there are diehards who refuse to surrender, and engage in acts of random terrorism—blowing up bridges and otherwise blocking reconstruction. Those who still seek social salvation through the state are such fanatical people.

CHAPTER 23, NOTES
1. Paul Johnson, *Modern Times* (New York: Harper and Row, 1983), 729.
2. Ibid.
3. Jacques Ellul, *The Political Illusion* (New York: Vintage Books, 1972), 3.
4. Ibid., 19.
5. Ian Hunter, *Malcolm Muggeridge: A Life* (Nashville: Thomas Nelson, 1980), 215.
6. Ibid.
7. R. Emmett Tyrrell, *The Future That Doesn't Work* (Washington: University Press of America, 1975), 3.
8. Ellul, 187.
9. James Skillen, "In Search of Something that Works," *Christianity Today*, 14 June 1985, 26-29.
10. Ellul, *Political Illusion*, p. 135. 11. Ibid., p. 186. 12. Malcolm Muggeridge, *Like it Was: The Diaries of Malcolm Muggeridge*, (New York, Morrow, 1982) p. 345.

PART
5
AN ADEQUATE
SAVIOR

CHAPTER 24
FANATICISM AND COMMITMENT

The twentieth century is the most credulous and conformist age in history. Modern Man can be induced to believe anything, provided it is dished up in the proper jargon, endorsed by the proper authority, or, best of all, seen on television. One of the reasons for this is that spiritual democracy is one of the major tenets of this age. All religious ideas are taken to have the same value.

Under the spiritual democracy, the Rastafarian belief that former Emperor Haile Selassie is God is placed on a level with the Ten Commandments of Moses and Incarnation of Christ. To say that one is right, the other wrong, is not acceptable. To claim, as Christ did, that there is only "one way" to God, is by this standard blasphemy.

Under current conditions, anyone can be labeled a fanatic for taking the claims of the Christian faith seriously. The early Christians were accused of being "atheists" because of their monotheism. Today's spiritual democrats show similar contempt for those who disbelieve that "all roads lead to God." This is thought to be fanatical, but the pejorative tag "fundamentalist" is often shorthand for "fanatic." Witness its use to describe, sometimes in the same breath, "fundamentalist schools" in the United States, and "Moslem fundamentalists," blowing up airplanes.

The temptation is to back off from one's commitment in order to avoid the labels. Worst of all, to gain "progressive" status, one may enroll in causes which have strong anti-Christian biases. No one is immune to these pressures. To press resolutely onward as the early "atheists" did is no easy matter. If one attempts to live out one's faith, state one's case or even take action on an issue such as abortion, then accusations of fanaticism will surely come. When they do, Bunyan's Pilgrim provides a strategy. He plugged his ears and ran forward repeating, "Life! eternal life!"

It should be noted that not even the eighteenth-century French philosophers thought that belief in the doctrines of Christianity constituted fanaticism. Voltaire even wrote *Treatise on Toleration* in defence of Jean Calas, a protestant, who was killed by extremists in 1762. Furthermore, after the Revolution, the National Convention ordered a marble column built and inscribed in memory of Calas, a "victim of fanaticism."[1]

The central issue, it would seem, is the difference between commitment—which even secularists admit is desirable—and fanaticism. The subject has occupied Christian thinkers for a long time.

In fact, early front-line fighters against fanaticism were Christians. Calvinist pastor Jean-Paul Rabaut-Saint-Etienne attacked fanaticism in his journal, the *Feuille Villageoise*. Protestant pastor Samuel Turretin published his massive (more than four hundred pages) *Preservatif Contre le Fanatism* (Preservative against Fanaticism) in 1723. He condemned the antics of Muntzer and John of Leiden, as well as early Quakers who regularly fell into convulsions. Turretin appealed to the "Light of God's word."[2] The question of authority is all important. The fanatic, or enthusiast, though he may pay lip service to the Bible, tends to see authority as residing in himself by some divine or mystical decree. Ronald Knox, a Catholic, insists that the Reformers were not men of this type and that Calvin's Geneva or John Knox's Edinburgh are quite different than John of Leiden's Munster.[3]

Knox also notes that when Luther and Muntzer squared off at Wittenberg, Luther wanted his opponent to prove his thesis in scholarly fashion, but found himself confronted with "men drunk with the spirit of prophecy." To the fanatic, the Bible is only infallible when interpreted by an infallible person, viz., themselves or their leaders. To the committed it has its own inherent authority, and merely needs to be clarified.

According to Turretin, the one who claims this special inspiration, "ceases to be in his proper mind."[4] The "prophetic" position is beyond reason and scrutiny, and therefore unassailable. The difference between commitment and fanaticism, then, depends largely on what one is committed to. Commitment is *sola scriptura*. Fanaticism is a form of personal infallibility. Accordingly, the committed person will be able to admit a mistake or change his mind; the fanatic seldom, if ever, does so.

Turretin also appealed to the light of reason. Of course, as a Christian he did not deify reason. Like Pascal, he believed that reason's ultimate step is to realize that there are things which are beyond it. But if commitment is based on Scripture, it requires understanding. Much of what has been called, often accurately, revivalist fanaticism in churches results from leaving one's understanding at the door.

The Irvingite movement in England was a forerunner of today's charismatic movement. Observers of the glossolalia and prophecy of the time commented that one did not scoff at it as drunkenness like the skeptics on the day of Pentecost. Rather, it bore all the hallmarks of lunacy. Thomas Carlyle was shocked to hear five minutes of unintelligible utterance followed by the brief interpretation: "Why will ye not repent?"[5]

These outbursts of enthusiasm fail as true commitment because of their transitory nature—the emotional fervors fade, "inspired" revivalists contend with one another, prophecy wanes, and schism begets schism.

Commitment, then, requires acknowledgment that God has given the spirit of a "sound mind."[6] Our understanding is enlightened, not eliminated. Commitment is anchored in Scripture and a sound mind. Fanaticism drifts; it is ultimately mindless.

Two of the most egregious examples of fanaticism in this book—the Munster and Guyana communes—involved a combination of self-deification and false claims of inspiration. All one need do to bring about a similar disaster today would be to combine the utopian socialist political ideology so popular among some groups of Christians with a charismatic form of prophetic utterance. Toss in a dynamic leader, a personality cult, a well-defined demonology, and the stage is set. There would be a long burst of glossolalia—and perhaps a vision or two—followed by an interpretation like this: "My children, thus saith the Holy Spirit. My kingdom has arrived in Nicaragua. Defend it with all your powers. Resist the structures of evil. This is how you walk in my will today, my children. Do not listen to the arguments of those who oppose you." It would not surprise me to see this happen, if it has not already taken place. A Muntzer may well arise from the ranks of "radical" Christians.

Fanaticism is noisy, public, and demagogic. Commitment is private, an affair of the heart. It works itself out in public but is fueled and rewarded in secret. Commitment is wide precisely where fanaticism is narrow. It recognizes a diversity of gifts and the various applications of those gifts. It is in this sense pluralistic while fanaticism is autocratic.

The committed person is able to follow the apostle Paul's advice: "Make it your ambition to lead a quiet life, *to mind your own business*, and to work with your hands" (italics added).[7] Fanatics, on the other hand, are very good at minding other people's business. Since their stance is elitist, they have no trust in Everyman. The fanatic asks, "Shall we call down fire from heaven on those who do not follow with us?" The committed person says, "Let them be."

Commitment, if it is worthy of the name, must be patient. It is a labor of love and carries on whether or not there are results. The fanatic is the one who wants great, sweeping, "structural" change *right now*! He believes that his own idiosyncratic gnosticism, ceaseless harangue, and energetic activism are capable of bringing this change about, even if there is no precedent for it in five thousand years of recorded history. Therefore, because of the unreality of his goals, the fanatic is usually profoundly unhappy, even though he smiles for the television cameras, which have a way of following him around. The committed often lack "star quality." But in commitment there is joy and peace; fanaticism can only lead to bitterness and *angst*.

What makes commitment difficult is its precision. It is specific; it loves its neighbor, an actual, living human being. Fanaticism is concerned with abstractions like Humanity, the Poor, the Aryan race, Structures of Oppression, Social Justice, or the Zionist Conspiracy. Commitment is individual, fanaticism collective.

The committed person, of whatever creed she may be, never confuses intellectual and social tolerance. Christians believe that Christ is the only way; they cannot then turn and persecute those who do not believe this. Indeed, they are commanded not to, but have sometimes had to learn the hard way.

But today religious people are more often on the receiving end of persecution. One of the most pressing cases of intolerance today, domestically, is the notion that anyone with religious beliefs must go straight to the back of the bus, shut her mouth on social and political issues, and accept whatever she is told or whatever is said about her.

For a biblical example of the distinction between commitment and fanaticism, take the much maligned apostle Paul. As a religious zealot, he persecuted Christians, often unto their death. In his mind at that time the distinction between social and intellectual tolerance was badly blurred. But as a Christian he lifted a hand against no one, encouraged fellow believers to do good to all men, and reasoned with people of contending positions. What made the difference in Paul's case is the answer to the wider malaise of our time.

CHAPTER 24, NOTES
1. For the entire inscription see Gérard de Puymège, *Fanaticism* (New York: Shocken Books, 1983), 86.
2. Ibid., 22.
3. Ronald Knox, *Enthusiasm* (New York: Oxford, 1950), 133.
4. Puymège, 22.
5. Knox, 555.
6. 2 Timothy 1:7.
7. 1 Thessalonians 4:11. Emphasis added.

CHAPTER 25
DESPISED
AND REJECTED

The real problem of modernity is the problem of belief.
—Daniel Bell

Whenever you see "no exit," it means there is an exit.
—Hugh Kingsmill

Observing the modern scene, it is difficult to avoid the conclusion that Western Man has decided to abolish himself. He eliminates his progeny before they are born, drinks and drugs himself into stupefaction, and often educates himself into imbecility. Having attained status and the requisite number of toys and pleasures, he often departs this life through an upper story window. Able to blow the earth into protons, he finds himself ever more insecure and impotent. What is worse, he has been known to praise his genocidal enemies like Stalin and loathe his friends—a classic death-wishing stance. A future historian will marvel at it all and perhaps shake his head in wonder.

The heart of the matter is that modern man, as Hoffer said, is going about his own soul-saving. Like the prophets of Baal, his quest for deliverance leads him to abuse himself. This is Self-Help taken to the extremity.

An adequate savior is what man needs. The Categorical Imperative of philosophers may be an interesting concept, but can scarcely be calculated to save anyone. The vague Life Force which has supposedly elevated our species from primordial slime to the dizzy heights of the Space Shuttle is too impersonal to have any effect. God as a kind of transcendent Senile Benevolence is too weak to earn confidence. The Advanced Extra Terrestrials who are thought to have started the Life Cycle on earth and whom some expect to someday return for us are the stuff of pulp fiction. And like the other inadequate saviors, they seldom elicit in their subjects what might be called love. No one dedicates symphonies to them, writes hymns under their inspiration, or undertakes works of charity on their behalf. For too many, there is no God to turn to, only Carl Sagan, [1] Isaac Asimov, and the descendants of Eleanor Roosevelt on the evening news.

Thus placed, they turn to themselves with adoring eyes. Or, they charge into the death camp of carnality and wait for the end, personal and collective. Some try to save the world by their own efforts. The blood flows and the bodies pile up.

Given the trend of fanaticism and the tools fanatics now possess, it is difficult to be optimistic. A neo-Stone Age rather than a neo-Fabian one may lay ahead. But for the living there is hope. The traditional channel of salvation may again be sought.

It sounds all too simple, but Modern Man's problem is not that he cannot grasp truths which are difficult; rather, he forgets or ignores truths which are too simple. He tries to live on bread alone. He returns God's gifts unopened.

CHAPTER 25, NOTES

1. Playwright John O'Keefe wrote his latest play *Ghosts* in response to the "theory of genetic fascism put forth by guys like Carl Sagan, who say that we're basically pre-ambulatory repositories of nucleic acids, manifestations of genetic stew." See Lawrence Christon, "Playwright Busting the '80s Ghosts," *Los Angeles Times*, 29 May 1985.

APPENDIX ONE
On the Treatment of Animals

The Bible does not support wanton cruelty toward animals. Christians are free to make up their mind about the merits of animal research, hunting and fishing for sport, and whether they will eat meat. The Bible, unlike the animal-rights movement, allows difference of opinion.

Though there have doubtless been abuses, medical researchers are not a cabal of Dr. Mengeles. Animal research is highly regulated, and much money is being spent to find ways to avoid the use of animals.[1] The Christian can applaud and support such efforts and, if she or he chooses, speak out and lobby against abuses in animal research. C. S. Lewis was an anti-vivisectionist, although a most reasonable one.[2]

But the only way the Bible can be used to support the animal rights cause as represented by PETA or the ALF is to eliminate the Fall. Everything created by God is for our use.[3] Moreover, Jesus chided the Pharisees for objecting to his healing of a crippled girl on the Sabbath.[4] How many of them, he pointed out, would take care of animals on the Sabbath, so it was hypocritical of them to prevent the girl from being healed. In this case, they cared more about animals than people.

Finally, a personal note. When Ken Myers of *Eternity* magazine assigned me an article on the subject of animal rights,[5] he said he wanted to get the piece published before some evangelical Christian came out on the side of the animal rights movement. This was about the time of the Baby Fae incident, where more concern was shown over the violated "rights" of the baboon than for the child. Something similar to what Myers feared has already happened.

A professor of philosophy at a Christian college was "deeply saddened" by the *Eternity* article. (Translation: he didn't like it.) And in a radio broadcast, Dr. Anthony Campolo of Eastern Baptist Seminary urged "pulpiteers" to preach against hunting. The people who hunt, he said, were "sickies."

APPENDIX 1, NOTES
1. *Bristol Myers USA*, January, 1985, 5, reports that remnants from eye surgery may soon be used to test perfumes, eye shadows, dyes etc., instead of live rabbits.
2. See C.S. Lewis, "Vivisection" in *God in the Dock*, ed. Walter Hooper (Grand Rapids: Eerdmans 1970), 224.
3. 1 Timothy 4:4, Genesis 9:3.
4. Luke 13: 10-17.
5. See Lloyd Billingsley, "Save the Beasts, Not the Children," *Eternity*, February 1985, 31.

APPENDIX TWO
Old Testament Genocide

Beyond the extremes of the European religious wars and the casualties of the Inquisition, there are clear instances in the Bible where people killed at God's behest. One thinks immediately of the destruction of the Canaanite peoples by the Israelites and the various other Old Testament holy wars. If anything qualifies as fanaticism, this seems to, as critics have never hesitated to point out.

For the Christian or Jew, these are some of the most difficult issues even though they are a matter of history, not news. The writers of the Bible certainly made no attempt to hide them. In treating the subject one could very easily write a long book; since that book has already been written, I chose to mention other examples of fanaticism by religious people, and to concentrate on the contemporary fanaticism of those outside of traditional religious faith.

Those interested in a most courageous and thorough study of the moral problems raised by the Bible, including the subject of hell, should see John Wenham's *The Goodness of God* (London: InterVarsity Press, 1974). Related works are referred to therein.

BIBLIOGRAPHY

All works referred to in this book are recommended for study on their respective topics. The following titles are the most comprehensive works on the general topic of fanaticism.

Cohn, Norman. *The Pursuit of the Millennium: Revolutionary Millenarians and Mystical Anarchists of the Middle Ages.* New York: Oxford University Press, 1961.

Haynal, André; Molnar, Miklos; and Puymège, Gérard. *Fanaticism: A Historical and Psychoanalytical Study.* New York: Shocken Books, 1983.

Hoffer, Eric. *The True Believer.* New York: Harper and Row, 1951.

Hoffer, Eric. *The Passionate State of Mind.* New York: Harper and Row, 1954.

Knox, Ronald. *Enthusiasm: An Epoch in the History of Religion.* New York: Oxford University Press, 1950.

Turretin, Samuel. *Préservatif Contre le Fanatisme ou Réfutation des Pretendus Inspires des Derniers Siecles.* Geneva, Du Villard et Jacquier, 1723. (To this author's knowledge, the work is unavailable in English.)

SUBJECT INDEX